TEAM DEVELOPMENT GAMES FOR TRAINERS

This book is dedicated to my son Andrew,
who at the mature age of five displayed all the team skills
I have attempted to develop in my work as a trainer.

Team Development Games for Trainers

RODERICK STUART

Gower

Published by
Gower Publishing Limited
Gower House
Croft Road
Aldershot
Hampshire GU11 3HR
England

Gower
Old Post Road
Brookfield
Vermont 05036
USA

British Library Cataloguing in Publication Data
Stuart, Roderick R.
   Team development games for trainers
   1. Management games   2. Group games   3. Work groups
   I. Title
   658.4'0353

   ISBN 0 566 07918 6

Library of Congress Cataloging-in-Publication Data
Stuart, Roderick R., 1938–
   Team development games for trainers / Roderick R. Stuart.
      p.   cm.
   Includes Index.
   ISBN 0–566–07918–6 (cloth)
   1. Teams in the workplace–Training of.   I. Title.
   HD66.S775   1998
   658.4'02–dc21   97–28404
                                                                 CIP

Typeset in Palatino by Raven Typesetters, Chester and printed in Great Britain at the University Press, Cambridge

Contents

Preface

This book is intended to be used by training designers when they are involved in team development programmes, and by trainers when they present such programmes. The games and activities are suitable for running indoors or in locations where it is possible to move outside and take part without putting on special protective clothing.

Given that the students on team development courses are most likely to have considerable experience of similar learning situations, as well as their own style of interaction with others, the role of the trainer is key to the success of the course. Team development relies very much on the complex and subtle interactions of a group of people, rather than on the learning style of any particular person. Hence the trainer has to be very sensitive to the feelings and attitudes of all concerned, and must adopt a facilitative style. For these reasons I have included some notes on facilitating adult learning.

Each game or activity has the following standard format:

- **Summary**   An optimum number of participants and a brief description of the game.

- **Objectives**   A list of the primary learning objectives of the game. Other objectives may also be achieved through each game, some of which can be seen in the commentary section.

- **Materials**   Lists any resources needed to set up the game.

- **Timing**   An approximate amount of time needed to complete the game, including all stages shown under "Procedure". However, in this context I would advocate that the trainer balances the use of time to maximize the learning on behalf of the particular group of people involved. He or she may wish to curtail a particular stage for valid learning reasons.

- **Procedure**   Details of the preparation in a chronological order. For most games it would not matter unduly if this order were ignored; the exceptions are where the trainer needs to set the scene prior to the arrival of participants (e.g. Candle Snuffing).

- **Commentary**   Explains the potential strengths and weaknesses of running the game.

- **Variations**   This describes variations which could be productively used.

Supporting materials

Since the prime purpose of using the games is to develop personal or interpersonal skills, I have included (see pages 253–267) a series of checklists which can be completed either by individuals or within teams. The completed checksheets can become part of a structured review which helps to confirm the objectives of the programme, as well as providing material for individuals to take from the programme as part of their personal development.

Design framework

I have also included a design framework which trainers may find of value. The first *diagnostic* stage involves two separate processes. Initially, some form of training needs analysis should be conducted to establish clearly the requirement for the development of team skills. Next, the trainers presenting the programmes have to establish the current skills levels of the individuals who will form the various teams. Once these skills levels have been determined, the main training stages can then be implemented, as individuals *develop* and *practise* the team skills. Finally, the procedure moves to the *application* of the acquired skills.

Thus the model follows a chronological sequence, a sequence which begins with a training needs analysis and ends with the application of skills in the workplace. This sequential strategy reflects the time-honoured approach: from deciding what needs to be learned, through design and presentation of appropriate learning experiences, to review and evaluation of the outcomes. The strategy is iterative in that the procedure would be continually refined and repeated to meet the changing needs of both the individuals involved and the sponsoring organization.

Acknowledgements

A number of people, books and organizations deserve credit for their inspiration over the years, and for their ideas which I have consciously or unconsciously incorporated into my own work as a trainer.

May I also acknowledge the unnamed gentlemen from the Royal Military Police Special Protection Unit, who charmingly ejected me from a training location in the middle of a game designed to measured competition versus co-operation. They explained that they had seen through my game, and would let me return when they had completed theirs! I learned much from this brief encounter.

I owe a considerable debt of gratitude to my wife Yvonne, whose continual support and keen sense of the realistic have often guided my ideas. She has endured many hours of playing management games when they were little more than ideas, and even spent a day during a holiday in Florida, together with my brother Colin and his wife Tina, working to polish one of the games in this book (Newspaper Chase).

The support and assistance afforded me by my partner Roy Preston has, too, proved invaluable. He has himself used many of the games and has found many additional twists and points of clarification to enhance individual games.

Finally, my thanks go also to Randy Gellner and Paul Nichols. Randy brought from his Canadian background a vital and energetic approach to our collaborative work, whilst Paul used his American charm and expertise to great effect. They both contributed many ideas and suggestions – although Paul did refuse to dress up in chef's apparel to make buttered toast!

R.R.S.

1

Introduction:

The role of the team at work

For most people, the work environment requires us to interact with others, so that we do our jobs effectively and in a way which is satisfying from a personal point of view. We share resources, work objectives, facilities, terms of service, special usage or forms of language, style of dress or uniform, and so forth. Hence, we are part of a group which has a shared set of goals and values, and as such we are well on the way to becoming part of a team.

However, when we as trainers are asked to design training and development events, the first and very important part the process is to identify specifically where the team has a role to play, and where individuals can make the most valuable contribution. For there are certainly many work-related activities that are carried out by individuals working on their own, and it would clearly be a waste of time and resources to design team development courses in such circumstances.

Moreover, many workers do not see themselves initially as part of a team. Thus when the need to develop teams has been identified and appropriate courses designed, it is necessary for us to take time at the onset with participants on workshops and courses to clarify the different characteristics of work groups and teams. Equally, we must address the issues of managing team boundaries, those grey areas of responsibility which lie outside the remit of any one team, but which contribute directly to the success of all teams.

Phases of team development

When involved in the design of team development programmes, it is worth considering the following basic questions to help achieve a logical, realistic and relevant programme:

1

- Do individuals have the necessary team skills?
- How can we develop any further skills that may be required?
- How can we review the effectiveness of the solutions?

In this book I have considered these questions in four phases: *diagnostic*, *development*, *practice*, and *application to work* (these phases are considered in greater detail on pp. 269–271). Here it is sufficient to say that the diagnostic phase covers the analysis of the development needs of individuals, as well as determining whether or not the work-related activities are inter dependent and the people therefore need to work as a team. The development phase concerns the evolution of the team, the practice phase comprises the rehearsal of team skills, while the application phase is the stage at which teams apply their acquired skills (most probably within a work context). This final stage is most important since it enables the effectiveness of the training to be reviewed, monitored and evaluated, and provides the link between the trainer and other parts of the organization.

People are people

Over the past twenty-five years I have been involved in helping to develop the skills and abilities of people in many different organizations. I have been struck by the common threads which run through diverse types of organization, and the common issues which they face in their working environment. Naturally, there are differing norms of behaviour, language, codes of dress and so on, but it seems to me these are eventually discounted as everyone within a specific culture accommodates to a special mixture of influences. They then seek to achieve goals and objectives that are remarkably similar to those in other cultures.

The development of the games and activities

I have used the terms "games" and "activities" to describe the contents of the book. These terms are intended to be largely synonymous, because you can make the games or activities competitive or collaborative depending on the objectives you are seeking to achieve. However, there are occasions when the purpose of the learning experience is associated directly with the work environment, in which case it would not be accurate to use the term "game".

A further dimension which you will need to be aware of is that teams can form from occupational groups, or from any other work-related or social interaction (e.g. a shared project in a personal development programme), and participants on your courses may therefore have met prior to taking part in a particular game. In which case, they will know each other and have some knowledge of each other's relative strengths, weaknesses, personalities, preferred methods of working, and so forth. In the book I have used the phrase, "those who have worked together", as a descriptor to cover such circumstances, and have placed this in the notes for certain of the games where it would be advantageous – but not essential – to select teams in this way. Where I have referred to "work teams", I am referring to occupational teams.

The activities set out in this book have been used in many different cultures, including the military, financial services, higher education, secondary schools, nurses, teachers, IT specialists, pharmaceutical managers, and so on. A number of professional trainers have used them, and have suggested changes to some activities which have increased their effectiveness. I see the games and activities as a series of vehicles through which people can enjoy a common experience and then explore, discuss and resolve issues that have arisen, at the end of the process applying what they have learnt to their work. The common experience enables an individual to develop his or her own repertoire of capability and confidence. For you as a trainer, the games and activities provide opportunities to develop a wide variety of skills and abilities through concentrating attention both on your particular objectives and on the needs of individuals within the groups. My suggestions about which objectives can be achieved from the games are a result of my own experience with them – you will no doubt find other equally relevant and enjoyable uses.

Objectives

As you will see, I have provided a number of objectives for each game (they are supplemented by the material in the design framework on pp. 269–271). Most of these objectives are self-explanatory. The exceptions are perhaps *assertiveness* and *influencing*, which both refer to forms of interpersonal behaviour. In my view, there is an essential difference: influencing is directional in the sense that the individual seeks to persuade others to act, whereas an assertive person may decide that he or she does not wish to influence others, and may even decline to play any active role in what is going on. Both forms of behaviour are however, relevant and important within a team.

Relevance to the individuals

On completion of a game, individuals must be able to make a positive link between the outcomes of the game and any actions that can be taken to improve the effectiveness of team members in their own chosen environment. This is important for two reasons: first, so that participants can apply the skills they have learned to their own environment (probably linked to their work situation); and secondly, in order that the training can be seen as directly relevant and worthwhile in terms of its costs to the organization.

With this point in mind, most of the games include a final stage where teams can plan future actions. This plan can be reviewed and evaluated formally or informally at some point in the future and helps to embed the training into the continuous development and improvement of people over time. From the training designer's perspective, this review data provides the starting point of another cycle.

Adults as learners

When we are involved in the development of adults, we need to recognize that every person in the team or group brings to the training event a wealth of experience. During my own experience of developing individuals I have come to appreciate that the learning which takes place is a combination of the content, the context and a set of uniquely individual characteristics that adults invest in the learning situation, as follows:

- their own reasons for wanting to learn;
- their previous learning history, including positive and negative learning experiences;
- their self-confidence, self-esteem, self-image;
- their learning style and pace of learning;
- their physical and emotional state, together with any learning impairments;
- their personality;
- their view of the world; and
- a strong need to play an active part in the learning process.

Facilitating team development activities

The role of the trainer is a very important factor in the success or otherwise of team development activities. It can vary from a didactic model where specific factual knowledge or skill is being taught (i.e. where the trainer's role is that of an instructor) to a free-flowing facilitative model where personal and interpersonal skills are being developed. At this latter end of the spectrum the role becomes that of an observer, reviewer and feedback of behaviour – rather like a mirror to reflect back to individuals their own behaviour. In this mode, the individuals are given freedom to be themselves, to act in a natural and comfortable way, and to take from this experience whatever learning they recognize as being relevant and valuable.

Individual needs versus team needs

Individuals will take from the learning experience what they choose, and they will certainly want to explore their own agenda. As the trainer, however, you also have an agreed agenda and learning outcomes based on the published programme. Most of the objectives of the team development programme are best satisfied when groups interact naturally. As I see it, therefore, there are inherent tensions in trying to meet the needs of individuals at the same time as those of the group. These tensions require constant monitoring and awareness if both sets of needs are to be satisfied.

There is a constant question in my mind when I launch teams into an activity: "When do I stand back and let all hell break loose as they go through what I would term 'the black hole to enlightenment', and when do I step in and direct them back to the objectives and outcomes I want to achieve?" One example springs to mind. I was running a negotiation skills game. Two of the three teams decided they did not want to negotiate, and instead secretly made a deal. These two teams appeared to get what they wanted, while the third team were extremely annoyed that they had been denied the opportunity to learn more about negotiating. I was obliged to review the learning experience for all involved, especially myself!

There is no single solution to this problem. I have learned, however, that whatever emerges in the review stages as important learning for individuals and teams must not be lost, ignored or glossed over simply to achieve – or appear to achieve – the trainer's objectives.

Forming teams to take part in games

I have also remarked over the years on the complexity of the issues involved in forming teams from groups. In the book you will find that the first requirement for any game is that you form teams. This bald statement can hide many potential pitfalls as you seek to put it into practice!

Often there are hidden reasons why individuals do or do not want to work with other people, which can cause tension. It may, for example, be an initial reaction as they meet for the first time, it may be a memory from past experiences, or it may be because there are others in the room they particularly want to share experiences with. To resolve this situation, I have found that using a random system of selecting teams – for example, alphabetic order of names, home towns, departments in the organization, and so forth – works quite well. Where teams have to be formed from certain departments, your selection process is of course restricted, as it is when you are developing skills such as the team leader role. However, in such cases I have also used another method of team selection, whereby you ask everyone in the group to form a line, with each individual taking up a position which reflects their own view of how much they know about the competencies being considered (e.g. leadership, communications, feedback, influencing, listening skills). Once the line is established, you have some indication of how confident each individual feels with regard to the competencies. You can therefore now form teams in a number of ways (e.g. from team members with similar levels of confidence, or from those with extremes of confidence), or select a team leader from the more confident end of the line.

The emotional impact of games

Taking part in games which are competitive raises the adrenaline level in many people, and the outcomes – where there are so-called winners and losers – can also increase the emotional state. Sharing such an experience within teams can be valuable both for the team and for the individuals concerned: for example, when they see a new facet of a colleague's personality, or observe the powerful impact of "group think". Faced with the likelihood of an emotional outcome, some trainers prefer to play down any competitive element by giving the events a softer title, such as sessions, activities, or learning experiences. You are the best judge of how to plan for these situations. There are many occasions when you will prefer the softer approach, but there are also important developmental opportunities which can best be explored through an explicitly competitive approach: for example, when you are concerned to practise skills such as influencing, team leadership, development of team identify, and the wider issue of co-operation versus competition for resources between work departments. A key to making the emotional involvement a constructive experience is to ensure that the review concentrates on the positive changes which can be made in the future by teams and individuals.

Developing team identity

One important reason for using games and activities is, of course, to increase the team spirit of work teams. Hence, anything you can do which helps participants to see themselves as unique within the wider group will facilitate this objective. The usual method is to ask teams to choose a name and logo that can be displayed on all occasions. Another idea that I find enjoyable and helpful is to use a variety of hats. Teams select those which they feel best describes them and attach a paper motif with, say, paper clips. Once the final review has taken place, both the hats and the roles that people have mentally adopted can be discarded, and individuals re-emerge from their experience to reflect upon it and upon the contributions they themselves have made towards it.

A sense of perspective

Finally, I firmly believe that when we are involved in team development, we need to keep a sense of our own relative lack of importance in the process. We may identify the learning needs, design the programme, bring together the resources, plan the sessions, manage the administrative issues, aid the processes, review and evaluate, and so forth. Whatever is learned during the interaction, however, is learned by individuals, and will be of value to them to a greater or lesser degree. We are simply the vehicle enabling them to learn – so let's enjoy the ride!

2
The games

Alternative Routes

Summary
- Suitable for any number of participants.
- Teams examine a map of a Roman town and choose routes through the town.

Objectives   Communication, decision making, diagnostic, influencing, listening, managing team boundaries, problem solving, team development, team leadership.

Materials
- Copies of team briefing for each team.
- The map of Municipium Aqua Vey for each team.
- Paper and pens.

Timing   45–60 minutes.

Procedure

1. Form teams and select team leaders. The task of the leader is to ensure that everyone is involved and makes a contribution to the team effort.
2. Two members of each team should confer with all other teams, to agree on what is an accepted definition of a route. The definition is recorded with each team having a copy.
3. Teams record as many routes as they are able to identify within an agreed time scale.
4. Two members of each team confer with other teams and agree the accuracy of all team lists. Announce the winning team.
5. Teams review their performance in private. The review should highlight individual contributions, decision making processes, clarity of definitions, and so on, and also how they managed the communication with other teams (similar to managing team boundaries with shared tasks and responsibilities).
6. You lead a session which summarizes the learning points to come from the team reviews as well as the links with work-related activities.

Commentary   This game requires teams to adopt a logical approach to their work, as well as a clear definition of what constitutes a route. If teams work out for themselves the easiest definition, in which a route is defined as moving from left to right down the map and visiting a unique combination of four locations, there are 56 combinations (see separate list). If they use other definitions, only they could work out the possible combinations.

The game is valuable for illustrating the different abilities needed within a team. For instance, some people will find it difficult to see a logical approach to counting the routes, while others will have ideas, but no influence, and so forth.

Variations   Give each team a copy of the map to look at for two minutes. Remove this, and give each a copy of the map with no written information. Teams have ten minutes to create the original map. The team with most accurate information is the winner.

Team briefing: Municipium Aqua Vey

This is a competitive activity, in which your team are asked to write down as many alternative routes on a map as they can from the North Tower to the South Tower of the attached map of the Roman city of Aqua Vey. Each route must pass through **four** locations (e.g. Grain Store, Military Barracks) identified by a bold capital letter. You may *not* travel north again after leaving the North Tower. The same four locations may be used in more than one combination (or route), providing that (a) the locations are visited in a different order in each combination, and (b) this point is agreed between teams beforehand in the route definition.

   The team with the greatest number of accurate routes is the winner. You are responsible for your own time-keeping and records of routes.

Reproduced from *Team Development Games for Trainers* by Roderick R. Stuart, Gower, Aldershot

Map of Municipium Aqua Vey in AD 159

		North Tower			
		A Governor's Villa			
West Gate	**B** Grain Store				**C** East Gate
⇐Cobbled Road		**D** Parade Ground	Forum		Cobbled Road⇒
E Public Baths			Sooth Sayer		
		F Temple of Minerva		**G** Chapel of the Eagle	
H Hospital					
				Public Well	
	Pottery kiln				
		I Military Barracks		Amphi-theatre	Burial grounds
		South Tower			

Reproduced from *Team Development Games for Trainers* by Roderick R. Stuart, Gower, Aldershot

Possible routes (56) through the city: Municipium Aqua Vey

ABCD	BCDE	CDEF	DEFG	EFGH	FGHI
ABCE	BCDF	CDEG	DEFH	EFGI	
ABCF	BCDG	CDEH	DEFI	EGHI	
ABCG	BCDH	CDEI	DFGH		
ABCH	BCDI	CEFG	DFGI		
ABCI	BDEF	CEFH	DGHI		
ACDE	BDEG	CEFI			
ACDF	BDEH	CFGH			
ACDG	BDEI	CFGI			
ACDH	BEFG	CGHI			
ACDI	BEFH				
ADEF	BEFI				
ADEG	BFGH				
ADEH	BFGI				
ADEI	BGHI				
AEFG					
AEFH					
AEFI					
AFGH					
AFGI					
AGHI					

The Amazing Electric Team Leader

Summary
- Suitable for any number of participants.
- Teams draw up a list of the actions that a superbly competent team leader would carry out, in order to achieve good team work, motivate individuals, and develop the team. They then add the actions individuals can take to support the team leader, and present their findings to the course.

Objectives   Communication, diagnostic, influencing, presentation, team development, team leadership.

Materials
- Copies of the briefing sheet.
- Flip charts.
- Pens and paper.

Timing   45–60 minutes.

Procedure
1. Form teams of those who have worked together.
2. Hand out the team briefing and ensure that teams understand it. Each team must acknowledge that any one of their team can be asked to give the team findings (see below).
3. Complete Stages 1 to 3 of the activity (see briefing sheet).
4. When the teams reassemble, select at random a member from each team to present their team's findings.
5. Facilitate a session to plan future actions that can be taken within the teams to increase effectiveness. As part of this process, ask teams to produce their own agreed action plan, complete with review date.

Commentary   This activity enables teams to move from an abstract model of a perfect team leader towards the type of leader most suited to their own work team. They are then encouraged to plan for improvements. It can be used towards the end of a team development programme, when you want individuals to look forward towards their work environment.

Be aware that the gap between perfection and present performance in the team leader can be a sensitive issue, and requires openness, trust and commitment from all involved in order to change the future.

Variations   None.

Team briefing: The Amazing Electric Team Leader

Working as a team, draw up a list of the actions a superbly competent team leader would carry out to achieve the following objectives, given that he or she has all the time necessary to do so, boundless energy, the combined wisdom of your present team, and the legendary persistence of a Scottish spider. The objectives of the team leader are as follows:

- To complete the task (this covers all of the work targets, goals, and so forth, that you are aware of for your work group).
- To develop individuals (that is, motivating each person to give of his or her best).
- To maintain the group (that is, to make sure that the group stay together, develop team spirit, and function as a team).

Stage 1
Each individual in your team should complete a list of the actions which the team leader would take, using the following headings:

- Task achievement.
- Develop the individual.
- Maintain the team.

Stage 2
Your team now summarizes these actions on a flip chart.

Stage 3
Finally, the team concentrates on the actions individuals can take to support the team leader in his or her efforts at team building. These are listed on a flip chart.

When you return to the main group, the trainer will invite one of your team to present the conclusions of the team.

Are We a Team?

Summary
- Suitable for any number of participants.
- Individuals complete a survey which describes some of the characteristics found in teams. They collate all scores to form a team total for each item, then examine the five lowest scoring items to consider how they can develop these characteristics further. Finally, they consider how to initiate new members into the team.

Objectives Diagnostic, presentations, team development.

Materials
- Copies of the team briefing.
- Copies of the team characteristics survey.
- Pens and paper.

Timing 30–45 minutes.

Procedure
1. Discuss briefly the differences between groups and teams.
2. Form teams of those who have worked together.
3. Hand out copies of both the team briefing and the team characteristics survey and ask each team member to carry out Stage 1 – first, completing the survey, and secondly, as a team, collating all the team's scores.
4. Teams now complete Stages 2, 3 and 4 of the activity.
5. Lead a discussion which concentrates on developing teamwork. One outcome should be an action plan for each team.

Commentary Valuable as an introductory activity for a team development programme. Many people do not have a clear idea of the differences between a team and a group, and this activity provides a description they can hold on to for future use. The activity can also be valuable to show changes as the team develops over time, by substituting a score for each of the four positions, as follows: *Always* = **4**; *Sometimes* = **3**; *Occasionally* = **2**; and *Rarely* = **1**. It is now possible to produce a nominal total for the team at a given date to indicate the current state of team development. At future meetings, the team should consider and agree documentary evidence to show changes for the twelve dimensions, and the survey should be completed again. The new score then reflects changes that have taken place in the interim period.

Variations   None.

Team briefing: Are We a Team?

Stage 1
Working on your own, score your current work team on the following statements. Add up your own score, which then has to be collated on to a master sheet showing the scores for all members of your team.

Stage 2
Working as a team, identify the five statements with the lowest scores for your team. Then decide whether your work team would be more effective if each of these five characteristics could be introduced or developed.

Stage 3
Decide how you would persuade new members of the team to maintain and develop further the characteristics you think are important.

Stage 4
Select one member of your team to present the findings of your team to the remainder of the course.

Reproduced from *Team Development Games for Trainers* by Roderick R. Stuart, Gower, Aldershot

Team characteristics survey: Are We a Team?

The following list has been developed by individuals on various team-building courses to describe the characteristics that they recognize in teams at work. For each statement, enter a tick under the level which you consider best describes your current work team.

		Always	*Sometimes*	*Occasionally*	*Rarely*
1.	We share the same "in-jokes", use of language and jargon	....	....	....	....
2.	We can be recognized as a team by the clothes we wear	....	....	....	....
3.	We are all aware of the team-work objectives.	....	....	....	....
4.	We feel accountable to each other.	....	....	....	....
5.	We share a complementary set of skills.	....	....	....	....
6.	We support each other and defend each other from outside criticism.	....	....	....	....
7.	We all feel free to express our feelings.	....	....	....	....
8.	We take pride in the work being achieved.	....	....	....	....
9.	We resolve conflict in a constructive way.	....	....	....	....
10.	Members are able to accept constructive criticism from the team leader or other members.	....	....	....	....
11.	Members voluntarily take on work of other members when necessary.	....	....	....	....
12.	Outsiders see us as a strong team.	....	....	....	....

To score your response:

    3 = Always
    2 = Sometimes
    1 = Occasionally
    0 = Rarely

The maximum score is 36, with a minimum of 0.

The Bayeux Tapestry

Summary

- Suitable for any number of participants.
- Teams are asked to produce a modern version of the Bayeux Tapestry, depicting their achievements over the past few months or whatever time they have worked together. This is presented on a flip chart to the remainder of the course.

Objectives Communication, creativity, diagnostic, managing team boundaries, team development.

Materials

- Copies of Bayeux Tapestry illustration.
- Flip charts and pens for each team.

Timing 30 minutes.

Procedure

1. Explain that the Bayeux Tapestry is a visual chronicle of events in the eleventh century depicting the progress of William the Conqueror when he invaded England in AD 1066. Hand out copies of illustration.
2. Form teams of those who have worked together. Where this is not feasible, use any system which, if possible, brings together individuals with some similar work-related experience.
3. Ask teams to create their own version of the tapestry.
4. Each team presents their version of the tapestry to the course. They are then asked to say what changes they would collectively and individually make if they were able to go back in time.

Commentary This is a creative way of making teams review their own development at work over a period of time. It is also valuable as a way of reviewing a previous stage of training. The outcomes of this activity can be displayed round the training room and used as material for planning future work-related actions that will increase the effectiveness of teams.

Variations Develop a tapestry of significant learning events during the current workshop.

Illustration of part of the Bayeux Tapestry

Source: From Winston S. Churchill, *History of the English Speaking Peoples*, i, *The Birth of Britain*, London: Cassell, 1957.

Reproduced from *Team Development Games for Trainers* by Roderick R. Stuart, Gower, Aldershot

Build Us a Crane

Summary
- Suitable for any number of participants.
- Teams build a crane to a design specification capable of lifting a predetermined weight. Points are scored for each of four criteria previously given to the team. The winning team is the team whose crane scores the highest number of points.

Objectives Communication, decision making, planning, problem solving, team development, team leadership.

Materials The following materials are offered to each team of 4–5 members:
- Copies of the team briefing sheets.
- 20 thin garden support sticks (about 5 mm square ended × 30 cm long).
- Sellotape.
- 2 metres of parcel string.
- 1 × 1 metre cane.
- 1 plastic bottle of water (2 litre).

Timing 60–90 minutes.

Procedure
1. Form teams, and select leaders and observers if necessary.
2. Hand out the team briefing sheets.
3. Teams take the materials and create their own crane. They can use the bottle of water as a test of their own design.
4. You score each design, then it is tested with the plastic water bottle and other weights as necessary until the destruction point is determined.
5. You announce the winning team.
6. Teams return to their own location to review their performance.

Commentary Teams value this game as a creative opportunity to formulate the solution to a problem which can then be practically tested. There may be discussions about what constitutes a crane, what are the rules for construction, and so on, which you may wish to link to work-related guidelines and imperatives. Creative methods of construction can lead to very high scores and provide ample opportunities for the team review, as does the behaviour of both the successful and the losing teams.

Variations   None.

Team briefing: Build Us a Crane

Use the materials you have been given to design and build a crane. You have 30 minutes in which to complete your design and building programme.

There are no constraints on the design of the crane (i.e. it can be free standing, fixed to the floor, fixed to the wall but touching the ground, and so on). At the end of the construction time, however, each crane will be tested to determine which team has developed the most efficient crane, based on the following criteria:

- *Distance* From the point at which the crane touches the floor to the point at which the load can be lifted. Each cm scores 2 points.
- *Height* The height to which the crane can lift the weight. Each cm scores 1 point.
- *Weight* The crane which lifts the heaviest weight receives a bonus of 20 points.
- *Appearance* Up to 30 points may be awarded for the aesthetic appearance of the crane (which is defined as belonging to the appreciation of the beautiful in accordance with the principles of good taste).

Note: Your trainer may offer you an alternative scoring system, in which a bonus is earned by the team which uses fewer resources. If so, the value of each resource is as follows:

String	6 points per 20 cm not used
Bamboo canes	10 points each
Green garden sticks	2 points each
Plastic bag	25 points

Reproduced from *Team Development Games for Trainers* by Roderick R. Stuart, Gower, Aldershot

Candle Snuffing

Summary
- Two teams of between 3 and 6 participants each are asked to blow out lighted candles placed about 5 metres away from them on a table. To help them they have certain equipment and a written set of instructions.

Objectives
Assertiveness, communication, creativity, decision making, managing team boundaries, team development, team leadership.

Materials
Two sets of the following:
- Written instructions.
- Lighted candles.
- Thin plastic tubing, measuring about 4 m in length. *One* length of the tubing has to have a connector fitted into the end, which can also fit into the end of the other length of tubing, so that it is possible to form one continuous length.
- 4 canes, each 1.5 metres in length.
- Length of string (4 metres).
- Scissors.
- Stockings or tights (one pair per team).
- Other miscellaneous items (e.g. bits of stationery, paper tubes, clamps, metal clothes hangers etc.). These miscellaneous items are not essential, but provide teams with possible additional resources that they can use to design creative structures to position the plastic tubing in order to snuff out the candle.

Timing
20–30 minutes.

Procedure
1. Without letting the participants observe, measure 5 m from the candles and mark this point on the ground. (Teams must not cross this line.) Place two sets of equipment side by side, ready for the teams to collect.
2. Form teams, selecting observers if necessary.
3. Give teams the following written instructions:

   You are required to blow out your candle, using the equipment provided. When your candle is blown out, all of your team must be behind this line. If you have any questions, these must be put through one nominated member of your team. You have ten minutes to plan how you will achieve this, and another two minutes to do so.

4. Teams collect their equipment, and begin discussing in private how to win the game.
5. When teams have planned how to win, toss a coin to decide which team goes first. Both teams attempt to blow out their candle. If unsuccessful, the trainer explains how by collaborating, each team could achieve the objectives very quickly – that is, by using the connector and getting the opposition to hold the tubing against the candle!
6. Team review their own performance.
7. Lead a discussion to examine how collaboration can achieve a win–win situation, and how competition for resources affects work performance, wastes time, and so on. Consider also the strategies of the teams and how they implemented them.

Commentary This game is a salutary reminder to teams to consider questions such as: "Who are our opposition?" "What are the problems of sharing resources in the work situation?" "What are our work-related objectives, and what is preventing us achieving them?" It is very effective when teams have a strong identity and want to succeed at the expense of others on the course. In the majority of cases, teams will compete. Occasionally, however, a participant will ask to borrow resources from the other team. In this case, simply refer the questioner back to the game instructions and note the complete intervention. Draw on it in procedure item 5 to illustrate whatever learning points emerge from what took place.

Variations Noughts and crosses.

Choose Your Own Sport

Summary
- Suitable for any number of participants.
- Teams consider a number of sports which could be used to develop teams at work and select four which their team would choose to play. They then plan and deliver a short presentation on their choice.

Objectives Communication, decision making, influencing, presentation, team development.

Materials
- Copies of the team briefing sheet.
- Copies of the illustrated sports sheet.
- Flip charts and pens.
- Syndicate rooms to prepare team presentations.

Timing 30–45 minutes.

Procedure
1. Form teams.
2. Hand out the briefing sheet and sheet of illustrated sports.
3. Teams complete the game.
4. Reassemble as one group, decide on the sequence of presentations, and ask teams to deliver their options.
5. Teams return to their own syndicate location, to review their team performance and contributions from individuals, and to discuss any changes they would now make to the way in which they would tackle a similar team activity.

Commentary In addition to developing the teams, this game can be valuable when you want to explore the motivation of team members and others at work. Assumptions of apathy or negative attitudes can be explored, as can positive ways of enhancing motivation.

Variations None.

Team briefing: Choose Your Own Sport

On the attached sheet there are illustrations of a number of sports which could be used to develop teams who work together. You are invited to choose four of these sports (or decide to include other sports) which your team think would be most suitable for them. You have 15 minutes only in which to complete this activity.

Stage 1
Consider the illustrations, and then list five positive and five negative points for each sport if they were to be used as a team development activity within your own organization.

Stage 2
Each member of your team is now allowed to nominate one additional sport which could go into the selection of four. In this case, the individual who nominates the sport must convince the others that it is a worthwhile choice.

Stage 3
In discussion, reach a consensus regarding which four sports the team will select, and place them in an agreed order of preference. Select one member to present your choices (aim for about a two-minute presentation) to the main group.

Reproduced from *Team Development Games for Trainers* by Roderick R. Stuart, Gower, Aldershot

Illustrations of sports: Choose Your Own Sport

1. American line dancing

2. Croquet

3. Ten-pin bowling

4. Cricket

5. Angling

6. Lawn tennis

7. Archery

8. Golf

9. Football

Reproduced from *Team Development Games for Trainers* by Roderick R. Stuart, Gower, Aldershot

Classic Cars Auction

Summary
- Suitable for three teams of 4 to 5 members each.
- This game involves three teams in selecting classic cars to purchase on behalf of their company. Given details of the car specification, team members make their decisions on which to recommend to the board chairman in a short prepared presentation. Each presentation is graded by other teams. On completion of all presentations, there is an auction to decide which teams have achieved their objectives.

Objectives
Assertiveness, communication, decision making, influencing, presentation, team development, team leadership.

Materials
- Copies of the team briefing sheet.
- Copies of the illustrations sheet of cars.
- Pens and paper.

Timing
60–90 minutes.

Procedure
1. Form teams, and select team leaders, and observers if required. Describe the format and purpose of the activity to the teams.
2. Allow five minutes for teams to decide privately how they would grade the presentation of other teams (out of a total 10 points). The points breakdown is not shared with other teams.
3. Hand out materials, and ensure that the teams understand the game.
4. Run the game through to conclusion.
5. Teams review their own performance.
6. Inform the teams that the cars are now to be auctioned. Each team can use the £200,000 allocated, and the winning team is the one which buys most vehicles. During the auction, each team can ask for a one-minute "Time-out" to discuss further strategy privately. (Hence there could be three separate "Time-out" sessions, with all teams frantically discussing strategy!).
7. Teams conduct a final review of their performance.

Commentary This game can be very effective in improving team presentation skills as well as the central objective of team development. The auction brings out a competitive element, hence there is a need to review the team performance during stage 5 of the procedure prior to this auction. The final review at stage 7 can be useful for the team and is a necessary "rounding off" part of the game.

Variations

1. Where numbers in the group permits – with over, say, 18 in the group – select four teams, one of which prepares a presentation to sell rather than buy the cars.
2. Substitute other commodities (e.g. houses, wine, boats, or the products/services of the company and/or those of competitors).

Illustrations of cars: Classic Cars Auction

The Winchester (British built) ⇒
10–12 seater
15–20 MPH
glass between passengers and driver
inflatable tyres
road sprung
petrol
£80,000 (API 5%)
spares ☹

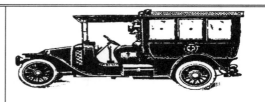

⇐The Oxford (British built)
10 seater
10–12 MPH
open top
solid tyres
coach sprung
petrol
£75,000 (API 10%)
spares ☺

Southern Belle (American built) ⇒
6–8 seater
15–20 MPH
glass between passengers and driver
inflatable tyres
road sprung
petrol
£60,000 (API 15%)
spares ☺

⇐ The Wayfarer (American built)
8 seater
20–25 MPH
glass between passengers and driver
inflatable tyres
road sprung
petrol
£50,000 (API 15%)
spares ☺

Berlin Grandee (German built) ⇒
6–8 seater
8–10 MPH
glass between passengers and driver
solid tyres
coach sprung
petrol-oil mixture
£40,000 (API 20%)
spares ☹

⇐Renard (French built)
8–10 seater
10–12 MPH
glass between passengers and driver
inflatable tyres
coach sprung
petrol-oil
£35,000 (API 25%)
spares ☹

Team briefing: Classic Cars Auction

Your company enjoys a niche market, hiring out prestigious cars to other companies for use by visiting business people from overseas. The companies have their own chauffeurs, who take the visitors (including their partners) on sightseeing jaunts, to the theatre, and so forth. In the past, most of your business has come from American visitors, but the market has become more volatile and the European business is growing rapidly. Most journeys are less than 5 miles, and never more than 10 miles. Each car can produce a profit of about 10 per cent of its market value. The attached pictures show cars which are coming up for auction soon, with the auctioneer's guide price. Your company has a budget of £200,000 available, but the chairman is emphatic that he wants value for money.

Team game
Your team is one of a number who have been asked to consider which 3 of the 6 cars should be purchased at the next car auction on behalf of your company. You must make a five-minute presentation (involving all of your team) to the chairman and others involved in the project. Your presentation should cover the relative good and bad points of each vehicle, your final choice, and reasons for rejection of the others. At the end of your presentation, the other course members will grade your presentation on effectiveness. Your course presenter may add another element to the game!

Key to car features

- *Inflatable* As modern cars, but with inner tubes for greater safety.
- *Solid tyres* Last forever, but shake the passengers causing the famous "jellied cheeks" effect.
- *Road sprung* Coil springs and central pneumatic stabilizers. Passengers speak highly of the ride, because there is no pitching or rolling present, just a gentle bounce.
- *Coach sprung* Solid, tested over a long time, and of robust construction. Very tiring on longer journeys (over 8 miles). Expensive to replace
- *Petrol driven* Can used modern (4-star) fuels.
- *Petrol oil mix* Similar to 2-stroke fuel. Needs careful mixing, and can cause nausea.
- *Profit margins* Each car produces about 10 per cent per annum in net profit in relation to its value (e.g. a £75,000 car produces £7,500 profit per year).
- *API (Annual Price Indicator)* This shows how much the vehicle is expected to rise in value per year.
- *Spares* ☺ Generally available, ☹ Hard to obtain. The cost is linked to the value of the pound sterling against foreign currencies.

Reproduced from Team Development Games for Trainers by Roderick R. Stuart, Gower, Aldershot

Cock of the Walk

Summary
- Suitable for any number of participants, with a minimum of 6.
- Teams consider an economics problem involving a gift to a friend and decide which of five options accurately summarizes the position on the gift.

Objectives   Communication, influencing, listening, problem solving.

Materials   Copies of the team briefing sheet.

Timing   20–30 minutes.

Procedure
1. Form teams.
2. Complete the activity.
3. Lead a discussion of the learning points which flow from the activity.

Commentary   There is no one solution to this problem, it depends on the perspective of the individual and possibly his or her work role. An economist would suggest E, whereas a book keeper would say A or B. A scrooge would suggest D!

   This is a valuable activity when you want to develop communication processes and skills within the teams during the course, since you would be able to record team decisions and the issues arising from different interpretations of the terms used. It is also valuable for looking at differing uses of language, perceptions and assumptions people bring to work, the influence used by individuals, decision-making within the team

Variations   None.

Notes for the trainer

There is no right or wrong response. It depends who you are and where you are viewing this problem from. When the problem has been given to groups in the past, the accumulative percentages of their average responses are as follows:

Option	Cost	Responses (%)
A	Nothing	34%
B	£10.00	11%
C	£10.00, plus interest	11%
D	£25.00	32%
E	(£15.00) saving	12%

Team briefing: Cock of the Walk

As an individual you are extremely generous, and have recently given a prime Rhode Island bantam cock to a friend. You had bought the rooster for £10.00 four years ago, and it could now sell for £25 because of its ability to cock and crow.

Which of the following options best captures your idea of the cost to you of making the gift? Produce a team solution.

A. Nothing. I had paid for the rooster already.
B. £10.00. The amount I paid for it.
C. £10.00 (the amount paid), plus interest on that amount over 4 years.
D. £25.00. The amount it would take to replace it.
E. Nothing. In fact, I am saving £15.00, since I only paid £10.00 for a gift worth £25.00.

Reproduced from *Team Development Games for Trainers* by Roderick R. Stuart, Gower, Aldershot

CommsAudit

Summary
- Suitable for any number of participants.
- Individuals complete a simple audit of how they see the communication within their own work team. Teams then review these findings and consider how they can become more effective in the future.

Objectives
Application, communication, diagnostic, listening.

Materials
- Copies of communications audit for all participants.
- Flip charts and pens.

Timing
45–60 minutes.

Procedure
1. Ask individuals to complete the communication audit.
2. Form teams of those who have worked together, and ask them to review the completed audits of individuals in their own team. The findings are entered onto a flip chart, and the team look for patterns of agreement. They then consider reasons for the particular result. These are recorded, including, if necessary, the name of any individual who appears to have a significant influence on this communication aspect.
3. Teams consider the future, and plan what actions they can collectively and individually take to improve the effectiveness of communication.

Commentary
This is a robust work-related activity where individuals have their say in the effectiveness of the communication within the team. Hence the second stage of the activity needs to be sensitively handled to avoid defensiveness becoming a barrier to improvement. Actions planned for the future need to be realistic, achievable, time bounded, and recorded for future review.

Variations
None.

Communications audit

Strongly agree	Agree	Statement	Disagree	Strongly disagree
....	....	1. We receive much information which is totally irrelevant to our work.	....	....
....	....	2. Much of the information we receive is too late for us to do anything about it.	....	....
....	....	3. Team members do not communicate with each other.	....	....
....	....	4. The manual/computer/written records available for us to refer to are inadequate.	....	....
....	....	5. Valuable information is hoarded by individuals.	....	....
....	....	6. Communication with other departments/divisions in our organization is ineffective.	....	....
....	....	7. Our team briefings are a waste of everyone's time.	....	....
....	....	8. We do not hold team briefings.	....	....
....	....	9. We are 'talked down to' in much of the communication we receive.	....	....
....	....	10. Much communication we receive has little impact: it is boring, dull and repetitive.	....	....
....	....	11. Unless an individual is actually there when information arrives or is discussed, he or she will not learn about it.	....	....

Strongly agree	Agree	Statement	Disagree	Strongly disagree
....	....	12. Much of the information we receive is not reliable/accurate/ complete/understandable.	....	....
....	....	13. We have poor methods of storing and retrieving information.	....	....
....	....	14. Members of the team have their own sources of information which they use and trust, but do not share.	....	....
....	....	15. We rely very much on 'the grape vine' to find out what is happening.	....	....

Reproduced from *Team Development Games for Trainers* by Roderick R. Stuart, Gower, Aldershot

CompuSpeak

Summary
- Suitable for any number of participants, with a minimum of 6.
- Teams decode a message which has been printed by a computer in a symbolic font, and reproduce the Roman alphabet. The game is competitive, the winning team being the one which provides the fastest correct translation.

Objectives
Communication, team development, team leadership.

Materials
- Copies of team briefing sheet.
- Copies of computer printout.
- Copies of computer printout translation.
- Sets of vowels (symbolic font plus English translation), with each vowel on a separate slip of paper. One set to be available for each team in the activity.
- Flip charts, paper and pens.

Timing
30 minutes.

Procedure
1. Before the game, translate the vowels in symbolic font into their English equivalents. Write each vowel on a separate slip of paper. Prepare sufficient copies for each team to have a complete set of vowels, depending on their requirements (see below).
2. Form teams, and hand out the computer printout and the team briefing sheet to each team.
3. Give the teams 2 minutes to decide on their game strategy. Then give each team a blank sheet of paper on which they can list the vowels they wish to purchase, and ask for a written list of any vowels required. (Teams not wanting to purchase vowels hand in the blank sheet.)
4. Give the teams the vowels they have requested. Make a note of any vowels "purchased" as a time penalty for the team(s) concerned.
5. Complete the activity.
6. Before commencing the reviews, hand out copies of the authentic English translation.
7. Review the performance of team leaders (if this has been one of your objectives).

8. Review the performance of teams.

Commentary As a leadership task this game can be used to provide an experience where team dynamics influence the leader. Some members will want to adopt a higher-risk strategy than others, while the nature of the task will indicate participants' degrees of commitment and capability. The game can also be valuable when you need to explore the effectiveness of different methods of communication.

Variations

1. When you want a short introductory activity (say, 20 minutes), hand out the translation as well as the computer printout. Then ask teams to write the names of their team members on a flip chart in the symbolic font, together with a short message to all other teams. One member of the team introduces the team, as well as the message.

2. Instead of using vowels to help teams, offer them a translation of the first line of the symbolic font, and if they accept, charge them 12 minutes time penalty for this support.

Computer printout: CompuSpeak

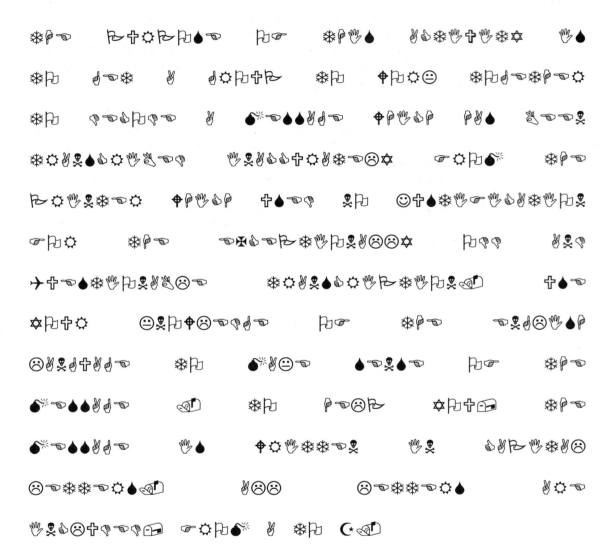

Reproduced from *Team Development Games for Trainers* by Roderick R. Stuart, Gower, Aldershot

English translation of computer printout: CompuSpeak

THE PURPOSE OF THIS ACTIVITY IS TO GET A GROUP TO WORK TOGETHER TO DECODE A MESSAGE WHICH HAS BEEN TRANSCRIBED INACCURATELY FROM THE PRINTER WHICH USED NO JUSTIFICATION FOR THE EXCEPTIONALLY ODD AND QUESTIONABLE TRANSCRIPTION. USE YOUR KNOWLEDGE OF THE ENGLISH LANGUAGE TO MAKE SENSE OF THE MESSAGE . TO HELP YOU, THE MESSAGE IS WRITTEN IN CAPITAL LETTERS. ALL LETTERS ARE INCLUDED, FROM A TO Z.

Reproduced from *Team Development Games for Trainers* by Roderick R. Stuart, Gower, Aldershot

Team briefing: CompuSpeak

Working as a team, you are invited to study the computer printout and translate it into English. You have a total of 20 minutes to complete the task, which includes 2 minutes to plan your strategy. The game is competitive: the team providing the fastest translation wins. If you so decide, you can "purchase" a translation of each vowel: that is, for each vowel "purchased", 3 minutes will be added to your completion time.

Reproduced from *Team Development Games for Trainers* by Roderick R. Stuart, Gower, Aldershot

Cooks' Dilemma

Summary
- Suitable for any number of participants, with a minimum of 8.
- Teams consult a suitable cookery recipe (e.g. see sample recipe) and establish a simple critical path for each stage of the cooking process. Other small groups score their efforts, and offer feedback.

Objectives   Application, communication, decision making, delegation, feedback, problem solving, team development, team leadership, time management.

Materials
- Copies of any printed recipe which has a number of ingredients and stages of preparation, plus different cooking times for each stage.
- Paper and pens.

Timing   45–60 minutes.

Procedure
1. Form at least three teams (both team B and team C have 2–3 members each; team A and any additional teams each have 4–5 members).
2. Ensure that all teams understand their own task.
3. Complete the activity.
4. Teams review their own performance.
5. Teams review their own workplace practices where joint effort is needed to complete a complex task, and identify stages of the process which can be made more effective and efficient.
6. Summarize the learning points, especially from stage 5 above.

Commentary   This is a good activity for focusing on communication within teams and between teams, when each team has a different task to complete within the same time frame. It is a practical activity in which to practise leadership or delegation, so that the team leaders should be briefed some time in advance of the general task. Applying the outcome to actual work processes can promote valuable ideas for improving work-related activities.

Variations   Any set of procedures which must be completed by a stated deadline.

Team briefing: Cooks' Dilemma

Team A

As a team, your task is to establish the earliest possible time that each of the cookery tasks can be started, and the latest possible time by which each task must be completed, in order for the meal to be ready at precisely 12.00 noon. An example of a task is that the carrots need to be cleaned and chopped. If there are any timings which are not given or clearly stated in the recipe, you should consult with a member of team B to agree an accurate timing. Be prepared to offer your solution to the trainer in 20 minutes' time.

Team B

Your task is to score the efforts of team A (and any additional team) that has been given the above task. You have to establish what criteria you will use to score each effort, and obviously you will need to be able to offer a perfect solution to the problem of earliest and latest timings. If there are any timings which are not given or clearly stated in the recipe, you should consult with a member of team A to agree an accurate timing. Be prepared to score the efforts of team A in 20 minutes' time.

Team C

Your task is to offer feedback to teams A and B as indicated by your course trainer.

Reproduced from *Team Development Games for Trainers* by Roderick R. Stuart, Gower, Aldershot

Sample recipe: Cooks' Dilemma

CHICKEN CASSEROLE
Serves 6

2 tablespoons light soy sauce
2 tablespoons rice wine
2 cloves crushed garlic
2.5cm (1 in) piece root ginger,
    finely grated
2 tablespoons vegetable oil
6 skinned chicken pieces, about
    100g (4oz) each
3 potatoes, sliced
17 ml (6fl oz) hot chicken stock
60ml (2fl oz) dry white vermouth
2 cloves garlic, thinly sliced
1 large onion, thinly sliced
2 rashers rindless streaky bacon
1 teaspoon Herbes de Provence or
    dried rosemary
1 teaspoon poultry seasoning salt
black pepper
4 spring onions, trimmed and finely
    sliced to garnish
2 tablespoons chopped fresh parsley
    to garnish

● Combine soy sauce, rice wine, garlic and root ginger. Add chicken, cover and marinade for 1 hour.

● Preheat oven to 190°C/375°F/gas 5. Heat oil in a large frying pan. Add chicken pieces. Cook for 10 minutes, or until evenly browned on all sides. Transfer chicken to an ovenproof casserole dish.

● Add potato slices to frying pan. Cook for 5 minutes on each side, or until evenly browned. Put into casserole dish. Add chicken stock and vermouth to dish.

● Scatter over garlic and onion. Finely chop bacon rashers and scatter on top. Sprinkle over the Herbes de Provence, poultry seasoning salt and black pepper.

● Cook in oven for 30–40 minutes, or until the chicken juices run clear when thickest part of chicken is pierced with a skewer and potatoes are tender. Garnish with sliced spring onions and chopped parsley. Serve hot.

Reproduced from *Team Development Games for Trainers* by Roderick R. Stuart, Gower, Aldershot

Creative Weighing Machines

Summary
- Suitable for any number of participants.
- Teams design and build a weighing machine which can be used to weigh a small item such as a shoe. They then weigh the item, and are scored by other teams on accuracy and on creativity, to produce a winning team.

Objectives   Creativity, decision making, influencing, problem solving, team development, team leadership.

Materials   The following materials are offered to each team of 4–5 members:

- Copies of the team briefing sheet.
- One coat hanger.
- Two plastic bottles, one full of water.
- Two small plastic bags.
- One wooden ruler 30 cm long.
- One metre of parcel string.
- One newspaper.
- Ten elastic bands.
- Ten coins (of an agreed standard unit denomination).
- One balloon.
- Paper and pens.

Timing   30–45 minutes.

Procedure
1. Form teams at random, and select team leaders and any observers you need for feedback purposes.
2. Give teams the briefing, and when they have understood this, allow them a short time to arrive at an agreed standard unit of weight.
3. Teams now establish an agreed set of criteria by which to measure creativity and accuracy (stage 1). Then carry out stage 2 in the briefing.
4. Complete the creative stage 3 of the activity.
5. Teams assemble again for the weighing competition. Each team weighs the items you have chosen. Declare the winner for accuracy.

6. Teams use the creative criteria to assess the design solution offered by other teams and score each criterion. Add the scores together to arrive at a winning team.
7. Observers offer feedback to the team leaders. This can be done as a shared session, whilst team members take a break.
8. Teams return to their own rooms together with their leader, to review their collective performance and the contributions of individuals.

Commentary As with many games which invite participants to be creative, you can increase the fun and flow of creative thinking by managing the prelude so that people are relaxed and comfortable with each other. (The way to kill the game is to have the senior manager teamed up with very junior, insecure staff!)

Variations None.

Team briefing: Creative Weighing

The purpose of this activity is to test your team's creative ability. You are asked to design a system which will enable you to weigh a shoe (or other item given to you by the trainer), using a standard unit of weight. Your solution has to be creative, so that in the final judging it gains most points for creativity and accuracy. You may only use the materials given to you by your trainer.

Stage 1
Work with the other teams to draw up an agreed set of criteria by which a panel of people could score a "creative solution to the design problem". The criteria need to cover all possible creative dimensions (including accuracy when it is used). The maximum score for the combined criteria is 20 points. Decide how you would allocate the 20 points between the criteria.

Stage 2
Work with the other teams to decide on your common unit of measurement for the weighing task. (A practical unit would be one which is based on coinage.)

Stage 3
Using the equipment offered to you, work within your own team to design a creative weighing system which will accurately weigh a shoe (or the article offered to you by your trainer). Your effort will be scored by other teams to determine the winning team.

Customer Clusters

Summary
- Suitable for any number of participants.
- Individuals consider the cluster of relationships they have with other team members that enable each person to do their work whilst gaining support, assistance, resources, and so on, from the other members. Individuals write down the support they need from others and the services they themselves can offer. Teams then produce a clustergram to show all the relationships, and decide on actions which can be taken to improve the effectiveness of the team.

Objectives Application, assertiveness, communication, diagnostic, influencing, managing team boundaries, presentation, team development.

Materials
- Copies of the briefing sheet for each participant.
- Flip charts, paper and pens.

Timing 45–60 minutes.

Procedure
1. Explain the concept of clusters by writing the names of all team members on a flip chart, circling the names, then drawing connecting lines from one person to another representing a link between the two names and showing some interdependence (e.g. sharing aims, objectives, resources, information flow, database, transport, filing systems, work load, and so on). As the clustergram develops, the strength of interdependence becomes apparent.
2. Form teams, hand out the briefing sheet, and complete the activity.
3. Lead a discussion on the actions proposed by teams, suggesting modifications to strengthen the actions.

Commentary This activity demonstrates clearly the interdependent nature of the team members, and any non-team players in the group. This may produce an accurate picture, or highlight areas of confusion or non co-operation which are impeding the team. On completion, you will have a diagnostic picture which can be applied to the work environment. Individuals can see where their strongest clusters lie, and also whether or not this is a reciprocal cluster. This helps to increase awareness and promotes further actions as necessary. It can also be used when you need to consider how to manage team boundaries.

Variations   None.

Team briefing: Customer Clusters

As a team member, part of your work is carried out by yourself, and part in co-operation with other team members. In order to complete some of the work you naturally rely on others to support what you do, offer assistance or resources, or perhaps check something for quality. They may carry out preliminary stages in the work, or complete what you have begun. However, you all have common goals as well as individual objectives to achieve, and you work within a cluster of relationships in the team.

Stage 1
Working entirely by yourself, write down three work-related areas of support that you need from other team members, and three aspects of support you can offer to them as your customers.

Stage 2
Working within the team, share the list of needs you have of others and what you can offer in return to your own 'team customers'.

Stage 3
On a flip chart, write down the names of everyone in the team. Spread the names over the flip chart so that you can then draw lines connecting names to represent links between yourselves as customers, sellers of services, common goals, time spent communicating with each other and so on. The completed cluster will show which are the strongest links between you and other team members.

Stage 4
Write down three actions to be taken within the team that will improve effectiveness in the next two to three months, and which can be achieved by closer co-operation and through sharing of aims and resources. Use a flip chart, and select one person to present your clustergram and action points to the remainder of the group on the workshop.

Reproduced from *Team Development Games for Trainers* by Roderick R. Stuart, Gower, Aldershot

Delegation Is Good for You

Summary
- Suitable for any number of participants.
- Teams sift through a list of do's and don'ts on delegation, and select five of each category to enhance their own skills. They then create a poster which could be used within their organization to promote effective delegation.

Objectives Application, assertiveness, communication, delegation, diagnostic, influencing, team development.

Materials
- Copies of team briefing sheet.
- Flip charts, paper and pens.

Timing 45–60 minutes.

Procedure
1. Form teams.
2. Hand out the briefing sheet.
3. Complete the activity.
4. Lead a discussion of the current general level of delegation within the teams, and what practical steps individuals and the team can carry out to promote more effective delegation.

Commentary This is a valuable way of introducing teams to delegation as a set of skills which influence their own effectiveness. The check list can also be used to review other games and activities, where, for example, you nominate a team leader for a particular activity, or the team are asked to nominate one person to carry out a set task or role.

Variations None.

Team briefing: Delegation Is Good for You

Your team have been asked to spearhead a publicity campaign to improve the skills of delegation in your organization. As part of this campaign, you have decided to produce a poster for the walls of all offices in your organization, and a plastic-covered *aide-mémoire* for managers.

Select five each of the following *do's* and *don'ts* for inclusion in the poster and on the *aide-mémoire*. Sharpen up the wording if you need to, and prepare a short presentation of how you will market the poster and *aide-mémoire*. Include suitable captions and any other visual information.

Do's and don'ts of effective delegation

Don't:

1. Apologize for selecting a particular individual. You have a responsibility to delegate.
2. Put yourself on the defensive.
3. Flatter any one individual. Balance aspects which are developed, against others which still need to be worked on.
4. "Pick over the bones" of work which has gone wrong. State the learning points for the future and move on.
5. Manipulate individuals by withholding information. Delegation is not an assessment, but a development activity.
6. Blame individuals for mistakes which belong elsewhere. Consider your own part in the process critically.
7. Criticize one individual in front of others. They will talk and not trust you.
8. Become judgemental. Using words such as "you ought to", "in my opinion," and so on, creates more issues. Focus on behaviour, and confirm the actions the individual will now take.
9. Threaten or use the threat of work sanctions.
10. Delegate work which involves making policy. That is your job!

Do:

1. Consider the individual's competencies level, motivation, and readiness for the task.
2. Be able to explain why you have selected that person for the work. Your reasons should include personal development aspects.
3. When you delegate important work, be aware of and try to reduce some of the individual's routine workload.
4. Plan an alternative solution in case there are problems of successful completion.
5. Be clear – and set out in written form – exactly what is to be achieved, the standards you expect, the timescale and so on.
6. Ensure that the individual can explain to others what the work involves.
7. Consider the effects delegation have for individuals, and be prepared to support them during this learning period.

8. Make individuals responsible for the work they carry out. If they make mistakes, let them know, but ensure that your feedback is objective and backed by specific examples.
9. Remember that delegation is part of personal development. As such, is a learning experience, and not an assessment of proven abilities.
10. If the delegated project is successfully carried out, praise the person in public.

Describe Your Work Team

Summary
- Suitable for any number of participants.
- Individuals consider some broad dimensions of a team and use adjectives to describe how this dimension is carried out in their current team. They then assign a value (positive, neutral or negative) to the words they have used. Teams draw conclusions concerning their own team from these descriptions.

Objectives   Application, communication, diagnostic.

Materials
- Copies of team briefing sheet.
- Copies of table of team factors.
- Flip charts, paper and pens.
- Space for teams to work uninterrupted.

Timing   45–60 minutes.

Procedure
1. Hand out the briefing sheets and table and ensure individuals understand these.
2. Form teams of those who have worked together.
3. Complete all three stages of the activity.
4. Lead a discussion covering the points in stage 4 of the briefing sheet.

Commentary   Useful for diagnostic sessions when you want individuals and teams to describe their work team, using their own language. The outcomes also provide a baseline for future reviews as the team develops.

Variations   None.

Team briefing: Describe Your Work Team

Set out in table form on the accompanying sheet are a number of factors that are found in the make-up and functioning of any team. These factors are recognized by team members, who use particular ways of describing each element. For example, for your team you could describe the factor "Communication within the team" variously as excellent, fragmented, slow, muddled, rushed, effective, speedy, clear, controlled, poor, and so on. (You no doubt have other choice adjectives you would use!)

Stage 1
Working on your own, list all the words which come to mind that you think apply to your work team for each factor listed.

Stage 2
Consider each word you have listed and indicate in the table whether you think the word has a *positive, neutral* or *negative* value as applied to the factor in question.

Stage 3
Working as a team, list the words used, together with the value for each. Then decide if each factor is generally viewed as *positive* or *negative* in relation to your team.

Stage 4
When you return to the other course members, be prepared to:

● Show the list to other participants.
● Give possible reasons why team members gave different values to the same descriptive word.
● Say whether you can describe the effectiveness of your work team in a general way from the words selected by individual members.
● Explain what individual members have learned from the experience about themselves and their own use of words.
● Explain what actions can be taken to move any negative dimensions into the positive value area.

Table of team factors

Factor	Words you would use to describe this factor as it applies in your work team	Value you place on each word		
		Positive	Neutral	Negative
1. Team management	....	....	....	....
2. Communication within the team	....	....	....	....
3. Communication with other teams and departments	....	....	....	....
4. Work achievement	....	....	....	....
5. Relationships within the team	....	....	....	....
6. Team identity	....	....	....	....
7. Conflict resolution	....	....	....	....

Reproduced from *Team Development Games for Trainers* by Roderick R. Stuart, Gower, Aldershot

Disappearing Golf Balls

Summary
- Suitable for any number of participants.
- Teams are asked to design a structure which will move a golf ball horizontally. They then take part in a competition to see which structure moves the ball the furthest distance. A team leader briefs his or her team, then takes no further part in the design or building of the structure.

Objectives Communication, creativity, delegation, feedback, influencing, problem solving, team development, team leadership.

Materials
- Copies of team briefing sheet.
- Copies of observer check list sheet.
- Paper and pens.
- Construction materials as listed in the team briefing sheet.

Timing 60 minutes.

Procedure
1. Choose a site for the competition. You will need a clear area of about 30 metres in length.
2. Form teams and select a leader within each. Also select observers (at least one per team). Take leaders and observers to the competition site, and brief them on their task without the teams overhearing (see team leader briefing).
3. Team leaders return to brief their teams. They then withdraw from their teams, but are available for the next 3 minutes to answer written questions. Observers remain with teams.
4. Run the design-and-build stage of the competition.
5. Team leaders return to their teams, and organize the transportation of their structure to the site.
6. Run the competition.
7. Observers offer feedback to the leaders. This can be done with all leaders/observers present. Team members complete the observer check list in a separate room.
8. Team members offer feedback to their leader, who then leads a review of the team performance. Attention needs to be on individual contributions, communication, team effectiveness, and the effect of competitive forces in work-related objectives.

Commentary This is a good game to use where you want to explore team briefings and the effectiveness of verbal communication. Usually, team leaders are able to reflect very accurately on where their own briefing was less than perfect, and team members on where they did not fully understand the requirements and then made inadequate assumptions.

Variations You can run the game inside a training location by substituting tennis balls for the golf balls (they help to scale down the distances travelled). This can become critical if teams design a projectile using the elastic bands!

Team briefing: Disappearing Golf Balls

Note: This must be an **oral** briefing given to the team by the team leader.

Our team task is to transport the golf ball the greatest horizontal distance, using only the materials we have been given. When I have briefed you on the project, I have to leave you to carry out the construction stage, but I will be available for just three minutes immediately after the briefing to answer any questions you may have. These questions must be written down by you, and I will answer them verbally and keep your copy as a record. If you see me again during the construction stage, just ignore me.

Requirements of the project

1. You have 35 minutes in which to complete the design and construction of the equipment you will use. This period includes the time taken up by my briefing.
2. At the end of this time, there will be a competition in a central predetermined location to decide the winning team. I have seen the place.

Constraints

1. The golf ball must be touching the top of the construction when it is released.
2. To qualify as a valid attempt, the construction must measure not less than 0.75 metres from the ground, and no higher than 1.5 metres.
3. The golf ball must be released by the tallest member of the team, using the left hand and with his or her back to the direction of travel.
4. Once released the ball must be allowed to come to rest without being touched again by any team member.
5. You will be permitted three attempts at projecting the ball, and your best recorded attempt will stand.
6. Should you want to change any of these rules, you must reach agreement with all other teams on this point prior to the start of the competition stage.

Materials
The materials available to you are as follows:

● Four sheets of paper.
● A small ball of string.
● Three garden canes, each measuring 1.5 metres.
● One golf ball.
● Twenty elastic bands.

There is only one pair of scissors available for use by all teams. These are held by the trainer.

Reproduced from *Team Development Games for Trainers* by Roderick R. Stuart, Gower, Aldershot

Observer check list: Disappearing Golf Balls

Note: This check list is to be completed by the observer during the competition, and/or by team members afterwards.

1. As part of the briefing, did the team leader clearly explain the following:
    (a) the requirements (to move a ball the greatest horizontal distance, using only the materials available); and
    (b) the acceptable standards of performance (i.e. the competitive aspect, the structural limitations, the operator restrictions, the "non-touching" restriction, the opportunity to renegotiate the restrictions)?
2. During the team briefing, did the team leader also carry out the following requirements:
    (a) delegate particular tasks;
    (b) ask team members to confirm that they understood the total requirements; and
    (c) answer any written questions clearly?
3. Have you any further observations on the leader and individual team members?

Reproduced from *Team Development Games for Trainers* by Roderick R. Stuart, Gower, Aldershot

Draw Us a Map

Summary
- Suitable for any number of participants.
- Teams produce a scaled map of part of the external location of their training environment and make a presentation to the remainder of the course on using the location for a scout jamboree or other outdoor residential activity.

Objectives Communication, delegation, feedback, listening, planning, presentations, team development, team leadership, time management.

Materials
- Copies of the mapping grid sheet (one per team member).
- Copies of the team briefing sheet.
- Flip charts, paper and pens.

Timing 60–90 minutes.

Procedure
1. Explain the purpose of the activity (which will reflect the objectives you want to achieve). Give the direction of true north.
2. Form teams of 4–5 members, and select any observers you wish to use.
3. Complete the activity.
4. Observers offer feedback on the specific areas of behaviour you have asked them to concentrate on.
5. Teams review their own performance. They should concentrate on effectiveness, communication issues, individual feedback to the team leader, and the contributions of individual members.

Commentary This practical activity can be adapted to most training locations where there is an area of ground available of approximately 100 metres square. It is non-strenuous, and requires team leaders to delegate specific tasks, monitor progress, and then collate the individual efforts of team members. It can also be used to review and reflect on the effects of having different resources to complete a given task (i.e. by making teams unequal in size), the issues of changing personnel, and so on. If you do use it for these latter objectives, it will be more effective if you explain this at the conclusion of the activity, rather than in the initial briefing.

Variations You may wish to introduce different parameters to the activity for the various teams, to illustrate the effects of, for example, time pressure, additional responsibilities, changes in personnel, new information, and so forth, on the team performance. To do this, simply vary the requirements in the team briefing. You can also remove individual members of teams at certain times and place them in other teams.

Team briefing: Draw Us a Map

Your organization has agreed to plan and run an annual scout jamboree in the grounds of your present location, and you have been asked as a team to produce a map that will help in planning the jamboree. To assist you, you have a gridded square on paper. Your trainer will point out the direction of true north, but apart from that, you are expected to complete the task in the best way you can.

At the end of your mapping, we need to know:

- The location of areas available for pitching tents.
- The positions of roads, their widths, and any potential problem points.
- Any water points.
- Any areas suitable as emergency assembly points.
- The location of all buildings in the area.
- Any problem areas for access by disabled people.
- Any points or locations which could be a hazard to vehicles or people.
- The total accommodation by type, size, and amenities.
- Any additional information which you consider would be of value.

Team members can apportion responsibilities amongst themselves as they wish, unless the trainer gives other instructions! When you have completed the map, produce this on the flip chart, and prepare a short presentation to explain your findings to the trainer.

Note: You have 45 minutes in which to plan and produce your final map on the flip chart.

Mapping grid: Draw Us a Map

Area: _____

Scale: One square on this grid is equal to _____ on the ground

Produced by: _____

Pencil in true north

The Four Seasons

Summary
- Suitable for any number of participants.
- Teams draw a set of pictures, depicting the four seasons of spring, summer, autumn and winter, to illustrate some of the experiences and achievements at work of various members of their team during the previous year. They then draw a further set of the seasons, to illustrate what they would like to see happen next year.

Objectives
Application, communication, diagnostic, team development.

Materials
- Copies of the team briefing sheets.
- Flip charts, paper and pens.

Timing
30–45 minutes.

Procedure
1. Form teams to include those who have worked together for at least six months.
2. Hand out the briefing sheets and ask the teams to carry out both parts of the artistic activity.
3. Each team presents their illustrations, and explains the reasons for each set.
4. Teams review their illustrations, and set out the achieveable actions they can take to help bring about the future four seasons they would wish to see.

Commentary
This is valuable as a diagnostic activity which enables teams to consider the recent past and near future in terms of what the team can achieve. It helps individuals to visualize their contributions towards the team effort. If teams find it difficult to see a different future because of lack of authority, resources, communication, commitment, and so on, ask them to analyse the actions which they plan to take in each of the four seasons and what others can do in the same time frames. Invite them to consider, first, whom they should approach within their organization in order to bring about the changes, and secondly, ways of approaching management, putting their case, and so forth.

Variations   Bayeux Tapestry.

Team briefing: The Four Seasons

Draw four scenes (synonymous with the four seasons: spring, summer, autumn and winter) to describe a typical period in the life of members of your team as experienced over the past year. Each scene can contain as many images as you wish to include, and the overall message from the four pictures should enable the viewer to see what took place during each season and how the year turned out. So that each scene is complete, be sure to include illustrations of what each member of the team did during the season.

Now look to the future, and redraw the four seasons, putting in what each member of the team would like to see happen during the year ahead. Assume you will all remain in the same team and continue working in your current occupation throughout that period.

Reproduced from *Team Development Games for Trainers* by Roderick R. Stuart, Gower, Aldershot

Go-Carting

Summary
- Suitable for up to 20 participants.
- Three teams work in collaboration to design, build and test a simple two-wheeled cart that can carry a weight in safety. The cart has two sections – the chassis and the bodywork – which are designed by separate teams. The third team act as co-ordinators and resource managers.

Objectives Communication, influencing, managing team boundaries, problem solving, team development, team leadership, time management.

Materials
- Copies of the team briefing sheet.
- Flip charts, paper and pens.
- One 30 cm length of string (to be used by the trainer as a cart harness).
- One 500 gm load (to be specified by the trainer).
- Resources as listed in the team briefing.
- Separate rooms for the three teams to work in.
- Suitable area (preferably with a 1 in 3 incline over at least 4 metres) for testing the cart.

Timing 45–60 minutes.

Procedure

1. Explain the purpose of the activity, which is to consider the way in which teams can be both independent and interdependent in their roles. Alternative objectives such as team development, team leadership, communication can also be specifically addressed, though these objectives should naturally emerge during the review stage.
2. Show teams where the cart will be tested (see item 6 below). Also specify what the load will be.
3. Form teams (which should, where possible, each be made up of participants from the same departments/divisions).
4. Allocate specific tasks to each team, and hand out the briefing sheets. (All information is given to each team.)
5. Complete the design-and-build phases.
6. Attach the string harness and arrange for the cart to be tested on a 30 per cent (1 in 3) incline. If this is not possible, select a location which will give the cart a robust test.

7. The resource managers report on the remaining resources on how successful they were in achieving their objectives.
8. Review the complete activity in line with your implicit and explicit objectives.

Commentary This is a practical activity which is fun to complete. It is of especial value where different departments take the view they are not part of a team but work to complete an independent function. This activity obliges them to consider the purpose of their department beyond this particular function. It also highlights work-related dependencies, and can help to correct misconceptions that departments may have about each other's attitudes, objectives, style, effectiveness, and so forth.

There may be certain assumptions (e.g. on final design, timing, use of resources, etc.) which need to be considered at joint meetings and decisions made on the basis of a common interpretation. Where changes are made to the "rules", they should be agreed by all teams and recorded by the co-ordinators.

The activity is also valuable when you are considering the issues concerned with managing team boundaries.

Variations Instead of loading a can of beer, you can use alternative weights: for example, a bag of pebbles or rice which must be loaded loose into the cart, a container of water, or perhaps three uncooked eggs!

Team briefing: Go-Carting

Your collective goal is to design, build and use a two-wheeled cart with one axle, capable of carrying a weight of 500 gm, and which can be pulled by a string rope for a distance of 4 metres. Your trainer will show you the object to be carried.

The design is in two distinct parts: (a) wheels and axle; and (b) the body of the cart. The two construction teams will each be responsible for designing and building one only of these parts. These two teams will be in separate rooms, and may only communicate with each other through Resources Control, who are the third team on the course. This third team are responsible for the co-ordination of the activity and design detail, and for the allocation, monitoring and costing of all materials used.

Resources Control team
Your functions are as follows:

1. *To co-ordinate all activity.* In order to do this, you must arrange meetings between the two construction teams. Only one member from each construction team can attend your meetings. Either team can ask for these meetings.
2. *To issue the resources to the construction teams.* Both teams can bid for (i.e. request) specific materials. Each bid must be accompanied by a suitable design. You approve the issue of materials against the design you have "signed off".
3. *To conserve resources.* At the end of the activity you must have saved as much as possible and handed out as little as possible. Your final 20 per cent of materials are your contingency supply, and, whatever happens, you must have at least 5 per cent of the value of the stores left at the end.

Wheelwrights team
You are responsible for designing and then building a two-wheeled single-axle chassis which will carry a 500 gm weight when it is transported over the test area indicated to you by the course trainer. The dimensions need to be appropriate to the load. You are responsible for the safe functioning of your final design.

Coach building team
Your task is to design and then build a cart body which will fit on to the axle and safely hold a load of 500 gm when it is transported over the test area indicated to you by the course trainer. The dimensions need to be appropriate to the load. You are responsible for the safe functioning of your final design.

Reproduced from *Team Development Games for Trainers* by Roderick R. Stuart, Gower, Aldershot

Resources available

The following resources are available from Resources Control, to be shared between both teams. The value indicated is the value of each item as a percentage of the total resources value.

Item	Value
10 garden sticks, each 300 mm × 5 mm diameter	20%
1 stapling machine with 20 staples	20%
10 sheets of card (A4 size), each being about as strong as a birthday card	20%
30 elastic bands	30%
1 × 1 metre length of parcel string	10%

You have 30 minutes to complete the design-and-build stage of the project.

Himalayan Saunter

Summary
- Suitable for any number of participants, with a minimum of 9.
- Teams make a practical survey of the training room in order to present a proposal to members of a Nepalese delegation (the remainder of the course members) who are seeking suitable training facilities. Much of the measurement is in Gurkhali language, using hands and feet as standard measures. The leader is given structured feedback by team members.

Objectives
Communication, delegation, leadership, listening, presentation, team development, time management.

Materials
- Flip charts, pens and paper.

Copies of

- Instruction sheet for Leader One.
- Instruction sheet for Leader Two.
- Course profile sheet.
- Window measurement sheet.
- Floor measurement sheet.
- Table and chairs measurement sheet.
- Walls measurement sheet.

Timing
60–90 minutes.

Procedure
1. Select two members of each team to be leaders, and brief each leader out of earshot of others involved. Give Leader One all sheets except the briefing sheet for Leader Two, who acts as an ordinary team member until the completion of the activity.
2. Ask all teams to complete the activity, and then present their survey findings.
3. After the teams have presented their survey findings, Leader Two in each team takes over to provide structured feedback to Leader One.
4. Chair a discussion to draw out the learning points for teams and

individuals, and their application to the work environment of participants.

Commentary As a practical game in which the team leader is presented with a great deal of detailed information and a task to be completed quickly, Himalayan Saunter is ideal for developing the skills of delegation and team development. Operating in the same room as others working to achieve the same task increases the competitive aspect and commitment levels. Equally, individuals are seen to be responsible for part of an inter-dependent process.

Variations None.

Instructions for Leader One: Himalayan Saunter

During the next 30 minutes, you are asked to lead a small team in a survey of this room and the course members who are present now. Your task is to supervise the activity, and then gather together the findings of your team and produce a summary on the flip chart, after which you will be asked to make a short presentation of your findings to the remainder of the course.

Background to the task
The Nepalese government are looking for training facilities in this area for their religious training courses. During these courses participants simulate conditions in Nepal, and transport all of the trappings and fittings from one location to another. Should this room be selected, all movable fittings might be carried to another training location by Sherpas (Himalayan workers used to carrying heavy packs up mountains).

Your team must complete a course profile, and, in addition, survey the room. Copies of all the instructions sheets are attached for your information. These include instructions on various survey items for you to hand out to team members as you delegate tasks. (If your team has fewer than four members, ignore the instructions for the walls.)

Should any of your team come to you for additional information or clarification, you can give this to them – if necessary, making your own decision on the information needed to complete the survey. Make notes of any decisions you make, and add these to your own summary.

You have 5 minutes to read through all the information, and then brief your team. Your 30 minutes begin when you start the briefing.

Reproduced from *Team Development Games for Trainers* by Roderick R. Stuart, Gower, Aldershot

Instructions for Leader Two: Himalayan Saunter

You have just completed the Himalayan Saunter activity, in which you assumed the role of a team member and carried out a particular task. Leader One now needs feedback on his or her efforts, and your task is to collate views from your team members and present this in a summary to the leader.

You have freedom to manage this task in whatever way you wish, and to gather the evidence in whichever form you think would be most effective.

You will have 10 minutes in which to gather and collate the data from your team members, and to prepare the summary, and then a further 5 minutes to present the summary.

Course profile: Himalayan Saunter

The Nepalese have asked for a profile of all members of this course. You will therefore need to ask all members questions to obtain information concerning their age, their height, how many sons and daughters they have, how many years they have worked in paid employment, and what skills they have. This information is collated and a final score obtained *for the course as a whole*. Ask your team leader for guidance where necessary.

Tick each box below, to get a total of responses for each box.

Personal characteristics
Note: < means less than, or smaller than; > means greater than, or larger than; *tuppo* means 'mark' or 'score'.

The following are the personal characteristics to be measured:

Characteristic	*Scale (characteristic = tuppo)*
Age (*purano*)	>40 = 5 >35 = 4 >30 = 3 >25 = 2 <25 = 1
Sons and daughters (*chora-chori*)	>4 = 5 4 = 4 3 = 3 2 = 2 1 = 1
Height (*algai*)	<4' 10" = 5 <5' 2" = 4 <5' 10" = 3 <6' = 2 >6' = 1
Years in work (*sal ko kam*)	>25 = 5 >15 = 4 >10 = 3 >5 = 2 <5 = 1

Enter the scores for course members in the appropriate column. Thus for example, if three of the course members: (a) are over 40 years old, enter 3 in the column giving 5 tuppo; (b) have two children, enter 3 in the column giving 2 *tuppo*; (c) are 5' 2" but less than 5' 11", enter 3 in the column giving 4 *tuppo*; and (d) have worked for less than 5 years, enter 3 in the column giving 1 *tuppo*.

Aspect of measurement	*Tuppo*				
	5	*4*	*3*	*2*	*1*
(a) *Purano*	.....	.....	.....	.....	.....
(b) *Chora-chori*	.....	.....	.....	.....	.....
(c) *Algai*	.....	.....	.....	.....	.....
(d) *Sal ko kam*	.....	.....	.....	.....	.....

Reproduced from *Team Development Games for Trainers* by Roderick R. Stuart, Gower, Aldershot

Summarize your survey by multiplying the total in each box by the number at the top of that particular column, and add the results together for a grand total.

Individual competencies and skills
Each member of the course receives *ek tuppo* (1 point) for each skill they can demonstrate from the following. To find the total *tuppo*, add up all the skills of all members of the course.

Skill	Tuppo
Charnu ko kam (Climbing)	....
Gari ko kam (Driving licence)	....
Ghora ko kam (Horse riding)	....
Naksa ko kam (Map reading)	....
Chitti ko kam (Report writing)	....
Kura ko kam (Any foreign language)	....
Total	

Grand course TUPPO
To obtain the total course *tuppo*, add together the total *tuppo* you have obtained from the last two sections – personal characteristics, and individual competencies and skills – to arrive at one grand total.

Window measurement: Himalayan Saunter

Note: When measuring, *take care*. Do not place yourself or others in danger. Make estimates where necessary. Ask your team leader for guidance if you have a problem.

Note: < means less than, or smaller than; > means greater than, or larger than; *tuppo* means 'mark' or 'score'.

Window measurements are made in *kadam* (hand spans). Place both hands on the window, thumbs touching. Spread fingers out as far as possible. This makes *ek kadam* (One hand span). Now you must find the total square measurement of all windows, in square *kadam*.

Having done this, give a score in *tuppo* from 5 to 1 for the total square *kadam*, based on the following scale:

Sq. kadam	Tuppo
>500	5
>400	4
>300	3
>200	2
>100	1

Enter the *tuppo* scored in the table below against **total window area**.

Now score the windows on the following aspects on a scale of 5 (maximum) to 1 (minimum) *tuppo*, using your own judgement where necessary:

- Cleanliness
- Decoration
- Ventilation
- Curtains (degree of light concealment, or black out, when viewed from outside)
- Frames (e.g. wooden frames = 5 points; metal frames are too heavy to carry up mountains, so only 1 point!)
- Direction (for religious reasons, 5 *tuppo* for facing due east, descending down the scale the further removed from that point)
- Security (5 *tuppo* if security locks are fitted, descending down the scale depending on how easily the windows can be opened from the inside)

Enter your scores in the table on page 84.

Reproduced from *Team Development Games for Trainers* by Roderick R. Stuart, Gower, Aldershot

Aspect of measurement	Tuppo				
	5	4	3	2	1
Total window area	.....	.....	.....	.....	.....
Cleanliness	.....	.....	.....	.....	.....
Decoration	.....	.....	.....	.....	.....
Ventilation	.....	.....	.....	.....	.....
Curtains	.....	.....	.....	.....	.....
Frames	.....	.....	.....	.....	.....
Direction	.....	.....	.....	.....	.....
Security	.....	.....	.....	.....	.....

Add up the total number of *tuppo* ☐

Now grade the windows on the following scale:

Grade	Total tuppo awarded
A	40
B	35+
C	25+
D	15+
E	<15

The grade you have awarded the windows is ☐

Reproduced from *Team Development Games for Trainers* by Roderick R. Stuart, Gower, Aldershot

Floor measurement: Himalayan Saunter

Note: When measuring, *take care*. Do not place yourself or others in danger. Make estimates where necessary. Ask your team leader for guidance if you have a problem.

Note: < means less than, or smaller than; > means greater than, or larger than; *tuppo* means 'mark' or 'score'.

The floor is measured in *bitta* (foot paces). One average-sized pace makes up *ek-bitta* (one pace). Ten paces make up *das bitta*. When you measure the floor plan, draw a diagram to show the location of doors and windows.

The floor is graded on the square measurement of *bitta*. Simply multiply the length by the breadth to obtain the square measurement (e.g. a floor 20 *bitta* by 15 *bitta* would measure 300 sq. *bitta*). Then mark the floor according to the following scale:

Sq. bitta	*Tuppo*
>500	5
>400	4
>300	3
>200	2
>100	1

Enter the *tuppo* scored in the table below against **measurement**

Now score the floor on the following aspects on a scale of 5 (maximum) to 1 (minimum) *tuppo*, using your own judgement where necessary:

- Cleanliness
- Colour (the brighter the colour, the higher the tuppo)
- Condition (new down to old in five gradings)
- Warmth factor (maximum 5, e.g. wood, down to 1 for very cold e.g. stone)

Enter your scores in the table below.

Reproduced from *Team Development Games for Trainers* by Roderick R. Stuart, Gower, Aldershot

Aspect of measurement	Tuppo				
	5	4	3	2	1
Measurement	.....	.....	.....	.....	.....
Cleanliness	.....	.....	.....	.....	.....
Colour	.....	.....	.....	.....	.....
Condition	.....	.....	.....	.....	.....
Warmth factor	.....	.....	.....	.....	.....

Add up the total number of *tuppo* [ ]

Now grade the floor on the following scale:

Grade	Total tuppo awarded
A	25
B	18+
C	12+
D	6+
E	>6

The grade you have awarded the floor is [ ]

Reproduced from *Team Development Games for Trainers* by Roderick R. Stuart, Gower, Aldershot

Tables and chairs measurement: Himalayan Saunter

Note: When measuring, *take care*. Do not place yourself or others in danger. Make estimates where necessary. Ask your team leader for guidance if you have a problem.

Note: < means less than, or smaller than; > means greater than, or larger than; *tuppo* means 'mark' or 'score'.

Tables and chairs are measured in *kuhunu*. The length of the average adult lower arm from elbow to wrist is *ek kuhunu*.

To measure the approximate bulk of each chair: (a) measure the height from the floor to the top of the back, and (b) measure the seat from front to back; then multiply (a) by (b). (e.g. height from floor to top of the back = 3 *kuhunu*; length of seat from front to back = 2 *kuhunu*; thus $3 \times 2 = 6$ *kuhunu*). For tables, use the formula: height × length of table top × breadth of table top.

Now mark each table and chair according to the following scale:

Kuhunu	Tuppo
< 4	5
< 7	4
<10	3
<15	2
15+	1

Enter the *tuppo* scored for each item in the table below against **bulk (chairs)** and **bulk (tables)** respectively (i.e. a tick for each item in the appropriate *tuppo* column).

Now score each table and chair in the room on the following aspects on a scale of 5 (maximum) to 1 (minimum) *tuppo*, using your own judgement where necessary.

● Frame (e.g. wooden = 5 *tuppo*, metal = 1 *tuppo*)
● Construction (e.g. assembled = 5 *tuppo*, moulded = 1 *tuppo*.
● Washability (e.g. all parts washable = 5 *tuppo*, graded down to 1 *tuppo* for most parts non-washable).

Reproduced from *Team Development Games for Trainers* by Roderick R. Stuart, Gower, Aldershot

Aspect of measurement	Tuppo				
	5	4	3	2	1
Bulk (chairs)	.....	.....	.....	.....	.....
Bulk (tables)	.....	.....	.....	.....	.....
Frame	.....	.....	.....	.....	.....
Construction	.....	.....	.....	.....	.....
Washability	.....	.....	.....	.....	.....

Where necessary, multiply the number of ticks you have entered in each box by the number at the top of the column. This gives you the total *tuppo* per column, for each aspect of measurement.

Add up the total number of *tuppo* ☐

Now grade the furniture on the following scale:

Grade	Total tuppo awarded
A	225+
B	180+
C	120+
D	60+
E	<60

The grade you have awarded the furniture is ☐

Reproduced from *Team Development Games for Trainers* by Roderick R. Stuart, Gower, Aldershot

Wall measurement: Himalayan Saunter

Note: When measuring, *take care*. Do not place yourself or others in danger. Make estimates where necessary. Ask your team leader for guidance if you have a problem.

Note: < means less than, or smaller than; > means greater than, or larger than; *tuppo* means 'mark' or 'score'.

The length of walls is measured in *pakhuro*. The distance between fingertips when the arms of the average person are stretched out sideways as far as possible is *ek pakhuro*. To measure the room, work out the *pakhuro* for each wall. Draw a diagram to show doors, windows, any screens or white boards, and remember to include these in your *pakhuro* measurements. Add together the dimensions of all four walls, and mark the walls measurement according to the following scale:

Pakhuro	Tuppo
40+	5
35+	4
30+	3
20+	2
<20	1

Enter the *tuppo* scored in the table below against **dimensions**.

Now score the walls on the following aspects on a scale of 5 (maximum) and 1 (minimum) *tuppo*, using your own judgement where necessary:

- Cleanliness
- Colour (the brighter the colour, the higher the *tuppo*)
- Condition (new down to old in five gradings)
- Reflective factor (maximum 5 *tuppo* down to 1 *tuppo* for no reflections shown)
- Washability (all surfaces washable = 5 *tuppo*, graded down to 1 *tuppo* for most surfaces non-washable)

Reproduced from *Team Development Games for Trainers* by Roderick R. Stuart, Gower, Aldershot

Aspect of measurement	Tuppo				
	5	4	3	2	1
Dimensions	.....	.....	.....	.....	.....
Cleanliness	.....	.....	.....	.....	.....
Colour	.....	.....	.....	.....	.....
Condition	.....	.....	.....	.....	.....
Reflective factor	.....	.....	.....	.....	.....
Washability	.....	.....	.....	.....	.....

Add up the total number of *tuppo* [   ]

Now grade the walls on the following scale:

Grade	Total tuppo awarded
A	60
B	45+
C	30+
D	15+
E	<15

The grade you have awarded the walls is [   ]

How Do You Manage Your Meetings?

Summary
- Suitable for any number of participants.
- Individuals complete a check list on how their work team holds meetings and the findings are consolidated on to a team flip chart. Teams then consider actions they can take to improve future meetings. A review is held after further team meetings to monitor changes.

Objectives   Application, communication, diagnostic, feedback, planning, team development.

Materials
- Copies of the team briefing sheet.
- Copies of the survey questionnaire.
- Flip chart, paper and pens.

Timing   45–60 minutes.

Procedure
1. Form teams of those who have worked together or who attend joint meetings.
2. Hand out the briefing sheet and survey questionnaire, and complete the activity.
3. Review the findings of the activity and record decisions made by teams.
4. At some future date after the course, reconsider the findings with the teams and evaluate the changes made to team meetings.

Commentary   Given that meetings take place frequently at work, and that they use up considerable amounts of time, this can be a valuable and relevant activity for a training course on team development. The activity enables you to complete a diagnostic survey of how teams currently perceive the management of work-related meetings. This can be valuable information and data for a training needs analysis. During the activity there are also opportunities for individuals to offer and receive feedback on their general contributions to meetings, and for teams to consider changes which would make meetings more effective. Ensuring that proposed improvements are introduced and maintained can be achieved by informal contact, or, more formally, by asking individuals to complete another survey at some point in the future and comparing this against the original.

The activity can also be used where teams have been formed to complete a project over a period of time and there is a need to develop the effectiveness of their team meetings. If you use it in this way, you may decide to ignore items 8 and 17, since these items could impose more formality on the activity than would be desirable or realistic.

Variations   None.

Team briefing: How Do You Manage Your Meetings?

Stage 1
Working individually, complete the attached survey questionnaire – marking each question on a scale of 1 to 5 – to give your own view of how team meetings are currently managed.

Stage 2
Working as a team, consolidate on a flip chart the views of all members of the team. This can be done either by asking members to call out their position on each item, or by collecting all sheets, redistributing at random, and then collating the positions. Each method has advantages and disadvantages.

Stage 3
Decide what actions individuals and the team can take to improve the next team meeting, and note these on the consolidated survey sheet for future reference.

Stage 4
After subsequent work-related meetings at a later date, the consolidated survey sheet should be reviewed by team members as a group to confirm that the changes proposed at Stage 3 have been introduced and are being maintained.

Reproduced from *Team Development Games for Trainers* by Roderick R. Stuart, Gower, Aldershot

Survey questionnaire: How Do You Manage Your Meetings?

		1	2	3	4	5	
1.	The procedures for calling meetings are clear/unclear.	Unclear	....	....	....	....	....	Clear
2.	The purposes of our meetings are clear/unclear.	Unclear	....	....	....	....	....	Clear
3.	Objectives for meetings are in writing or we set an agreed agenda.	Seldom	....	....	....	....	....	Usually
4.	All members can add to the agenda before the meeting.	Seldom	....	....	....	....	....	Usually
5.	Meetings start and finish on time.	Seldom	....	....	....	....	....	Usually
6.	Everyone who needs to attend actually does so.	Seldom	....	....	....	....	....	Usually
7.	We have a nominated chair person who acts with agreement.	Seldom	....	....	....	....	....	Usually
8.	Effective training is given on chairing meetings.	Seldom	....	....	....	....	....	Usually
9.	There is a written record of decisions made.	Seldom	....	....	....	....	....	Usually
10.	There is a positive atmosphere in our meetings.	Seldom	....	....	....	....	....	Usually
11.	Members are given time to make their contributions to the meeting.	Seldom	....	....	....	....	....	Usually
12.	Clear summaries are made during the meetings.	Seldom	....	....	....	....	....	Usually
13.	Meetings concentrate on achieving solutions, not on attaching blame for past failures.	Seldom	....	....	....	....	....	Usually
14.	Individuals receive feedback on the effectiveness of their contributions.	Seldom	....	....	....	....	....	Usually
15.	Decisions made are followed up at our next meeting.	Seldom	....	....	....	....	....	Usually
16.	Meetings make the best use of everyone's time.	Seldom	....	....	....	....	....	Usually
17.	Meetings are reviewed to see what changes need to be made.	Seldom	....	....	....	....	....	Usually
18.	Methods of informing external agencies, individuals and departments of decisions taken are clear/unclear	Unclear	....	....	....	....	....	Clear

Reproduced from *Team Development Games for Trainers* by Roderick R. Stuart, Gower, Aldershot

How Healthy Is the Patient?

Summary
- Suitable for any number of participants.
- Teams consider their own working practices over the past six months from the viewpoint of physicians diagnosing health. Observations of behaviour to resolve conflict within the team are recorded on a flip chart under two headings: *poor* and *good* health. Teams report back on their findings.

Objectives Communication, conflict management, diagnostic, team development.

Materials
- Copies of the team briefing sheet.
- Flip charts, paper and pens.

Timing 45–60 minutes.

Procedure
1. Form teams of those who have worked together recently.
2. Complete the activity.
3. Invite teams to make a short presentation of their findings and recommendations for future action.
4. Lead a discussion focusing on conflict management within teams.

Commentary This activity can be used in two distinct ways: first, as a review of how the teams have handled conflict during their working relationships; secondly, as a review of other competitive games and activities within this book. Conflict will arise within teams during these games and activities, and some of the behaviours described in this briefing sheet will take place. Whichever approach is used, however, the value for participants will come when they recognize the relationship between their own conflict management and overall team health.

You may wish to use this activity as a process review of a particular game, and revisit it during the final session when looking forward to future actions in the workplace.

Variations None.

Team briefing: How Healthy Is the Patient?

When teams are observed from the outside, it is sometimes very easy to see that they are in poor health as a working unit. One symptom of health is the way conflict is handled, as shown in the following table:

Poor health	*Good health*
Where conflict is present team members may:	Where conflict is resolved successfully, team members may:
<ul><li>Withdraw physically or mentally from the team.</li><li>Take sides in discussing issues.</li><li>"Send people to Coventry."</li><li>Gossip, using indirect "coded" language not shared with other team members.</li><li>Indulge in petty practical jokes.</li><li>Devote time and energy to obstructing team work.</li></ul>	<ul><li>Adopt a win–win focus.</li><li>Contribute to an overall solution.</li><li>Actively support other team members.</li><li>Use a common language that emphasizes team identity.</li><li>Develop team banter towards other groups.</li><li>Carry out willingly any part of the team work that needs to be done.</li></ul>

Stage 1
Working as a team, diagnose your own team health during the past six months or so. Use two flip charts marked GOOD and POOR to record instances when individual members or all of your team have behaved in ways which lead you to conclude that the patient (your work team) is in good or ill health. As well as recording the behaviour, look for reasons to explain it.

Stage 2
Agree on the "medicine" you would prescribe to improve the health of the patient. Your medicine may include, for example, different behaviours by team members, or by others outside the team, additional training or development, and any support you think the team needs from others in the organization.

Stage 3
Write your observations on a flip chart, and select one member of the team to present this to the whole course. Having completed your observations list, create a light-hearted but apt description of how you all feel about the health of the patient. This can also be offered to other course members.

Leadership Styles and Values

Summary
- Suitable for any number of participants.
- Individuals complete an inventory based on the functional approach to leadership. They then compare their preferred style with others in the team and consider the relative effectiveness of the style in terms of the values within the work team and the organization.

Objectives   Diagnostic, team development, team leadership.

Materials
- Copies of the style of management survey sheet.
- Copies of the individual briefing.
- Flip charts, paper and pens.

Timing   45–60 minutes.

Procedure
1. Form teams. Then hand out the briefing and survey sheets, and ask team members to complete the survey sheet individually.
2. Teams consider the resulting preferred styles to answer three questions:
   (a) Is there a common preferred style in the team?
   (b) Which style would result in the team being most effective?
   (c) What actions could be taken within the team to change the present style to the most effective style?
3. Bring the teams together and lead a discussion on the findings from item 2 above.

Commentary   This activity can also be used to diagnose the values promoted within the organization, by asking individuals to complete the survey as an audit of what they think happens at present (i.e. which of the three options for each statement would our managers be expected to use, or gain promotion through using?). This can be compared with the preferred styles of individuals and teams.

Variations   None.

Individual briefing: Leadership Styles and Values

Preferred style of team leadership
First, think about yourself as a team member, and how you would wish to be managed by your line manager, supervisor or team leader.

The attached style of management survey will enable you to reflect on your own preferred style of managing and of being managed. Secondly, therefore, consider the statements in the survey and analyse each set in order of importance, by entering the letters – **a, b, c,** – in the appropriate boxes. Thus in the first set:

a Ensure that the task is completed on time.
b Deal rapidly with personal problems of individuals.
c Ensure that all group members are treated equally.

If your chosen order of importance is **b, a, c** (the most important being **b**, and the least important, **c**), the completed box would read:

5	3	1
b	a	c

Next, add up your total score for each letter. This will indicate to you how you prefer a leader to act (see below), and, by inference, the relative scores you give to the various activities. These relative scores may also reflect the style of management you would prefer to adopt, given the leadership role.

Functions of management
Letter **a** deals with the *task* function of a manager. The activities uppermost in the mind of a leader who concentrates on the task would be as follows:

● Defining the task.
● Making a plan.
● Allocating work and resources.
● Controlling the tempo and quality of work.
● Checking performance against the plan.
● Adjusting the plan as necessary.

Letter **b** deals with the *individual* functions, and the type of activities here are the following:

Reproduced from Team Development Games for Trainers by Roderick R. Stuart, Gower, Aldershot

- Attending to personal problems.
- Encouraging individuals.
- Giving status.
- Recognizing and using individual abilities.
- Training the individual.

Letter **c** involves the *group* function of a manager, and includes the following activities:

- Building team spirit and identity.
- Setting standards.
- Maintaining discipline within the group.
- Encouraging and motivating throughout the group.
- Giving a sense of purpose to the group.
- Ensuring effective communication within the group.

The maximum score in any one of the three categories – **a, b** and **c** – is 75, and the minimum is 15.

If your personal score is low in one of the categories, perhaps you should consider why this is. In a practical leadership role, all three sets of activities have to be managed, and to neglect any one category will sooner or later lead to problems.

You may also decide on reflection that in some work situations you should operate differently, which would change the balance of your scores in the three categories. This demonstrates your ability to manage effectively! However, you may still have a preferred style of *being a follower*!

Note: The origins of this approach to leadership go back to at least 1948, when it was seen as a two-dimensional model. Since then, the British Army developed it as the *functional approach*, during the 1960s and 1970s. Professor John Adair has also been responsible for introducing the model into many different organizations.

Reproduced from *Team Development Games for Trainers* by Roderick R. Stuart, Gower, Aldershot

Preferred style of management survey: Leadership Styles and Values

1. **a** Ensure that the task is completed on time.
   b Deal rapidly with personal problems of individuals.
   c Ensure that all group members are treated equally.

5	3	1

2. **a** Tell each individual exactly what they must do.
   b Discuss with individuals their role in the task.
   c Ensure good communication within the group.

5	3	1

3. **a** Decide the best course of action.
   b Consult individuals and let them contribute ideas.
   c Let the team decide what is to be done.

5	3	1

4. **a** Allocate tasks to individuals.
   b Encourage individuals to select their own tasks.
   c Let the team decide who does what task.

5	3	1

5. **a** Maintain firm discipline in the group.
   b Expect individuals to be self-disciplined.
   c Seek group consensus for standards of behaviour.

5	3	1

6. **a** Assume that the completed task is sufficient reward.
   b Thank individuals when alone with them.
   c Publicly praise the team for their joint efforts.

5	3	1

7. **a** Take the blame for failures.
   b Look for individual weaknesses.
   c Focus on group responsibility for the failure.

5	3	1

8. **a** Use only those skills which achieve task completion.
   b Support individuals to develops their own range of skills.
   c Focus on the development of complementary team roles.

5	3	1

9. **a** Measure achievements in relation to the work in hand.
   b Measure achievements in relation to the individual's experience.
   c Measure achievements in relation to the expected group standards.

5	3	1

Reproduced from *Team Development Games for Trainers* by Roderick R. Stuart, Gower, Aldershot

10. a Make work a higher priority than the needs of
       individuals.
    b Change work patterns to meet the needs of individuals.
    c Make individuals conform with the group work
       pattern.

5	3	1

11. a Tightly control the progress of work completion.
    b Expect individuals to meet their own deadlines.
    c Co-opt group help in exerting pressure on individuals
       to meet deadlines.

5	3	1

12. a Personally evaluate the completion of the task for the
       group.
    b Ask individuals to assess their own performance.
    c Expect the group to evaluate its own performance.

5	3	1

13. a Obtain whatever resources are needed himself/herself.
    b Nominate an individual to obtain resources needed.
    c Let the group decide and requisition the resources
       needed.

5	3	1

14. a Plan exactly what the team must accomplish.
    b Let individuals decide the plan of action.
    c Seek group agreement to the plan.

5	3	1

15. a Leave personal relations out of all work situations.
    b Get to know you as an individual.
    c Concentrate on building the team as a social group.

5	3	1

Reproduced from *Team Development Games for Trainers* by Roderick R. Stuart, Gower, Aldershot

Like the Hat?

Summary
- Suitable for any number of participants.
- Teams from several departments in an organization work together to establish how they are interdependent and make a valuable contribution to organizational goals. Fun is an important aspect of this activity.

Objectives Assertiveness, communication, diagnostic, influencing, managing team boundaries, presentations, team development.

Materials
- Materials to make hats (newspapers, flip-chart paper, sellotape, staples etc.).
- Copies of the team briefing sheet.
- Flip charts, paper and pens.

Timing 45–60 minutes.

Procedure
1. Explain the purpose of the activity, which is to demonstrate the importance of each department and the interdependence relationship.
2. Participants pair up with someone from another department, and spend 10 minutes writing down on a flip chart their own endings to the phrase "You'll miss us when we're gone because ...".
3. These are quickly communicated to the whole group.
4. Each department then produces the following:
   (a) a slogan for use within the organization: "You'll miss us when we're gone, because ...";
   (b) a hat which could be used within the department to safeguard the wearer from flying brickbats arriving from other departments.
5. The whole course regroup and draw a chart over at least two linked sheets of flip-chart paper. The chart has circles for each department, with their slogan inscribed within their respective circle, and the task of the group is to draw lines connecting the circles which represent interdepartmental communication, shared objectives, shared resources, time spent working together, shared database, transport, IT systems and any other aspect of work they share.

Every department must be clearly shown to support the organizational team network.

6. The whole group make a presentation describing the network. This is done by departmental representatives. The first three representatives stand in a line in front of the trainer, wearing their hats. The right-hand person briefly describes his or her own contribution on the network diagram, explains why their hat is designed in a particular way, and then sits down. The next representative in line on the right takes his or her place, and another departmental representative joins the line on the left, complete with department hat.

7. At the end of this process each department in closed session reviews its contribution to the network, and decides on *three* actions it can take to improve the effectiveness of its team contribution.

8. Following this review, all departments offer their ideas on this subject to the whole course.

Commentary This is a valuable activity to use where different departments have the view they are not part of a team, but work to complete an independent function. The activity obliges each of them to consider the purpose of their department beyond this function. It also highlights work-related dependencies, and can help to correct misconceptions that departments may have about each other's attitudes, objectives, style, effectiveness, and so forth. You may also find the activity useful in addressing the issue of communicating across team boundaries. The hats are a useful symbol through which issues can be channelled, and provide opportunities for the fun element. The initial pairing for stage two often results from friendship rather than work-related reasons. This can help to ease tensions, and has no adverse bearing on the activity.

Variations None.

Team briefing: Like the Hat?

1. Working as a department of your own organization, create:
   (a) a slogan starting: "You'll miss us when we're gone, because...", which should capture the essential aim of your departmental work role in the organization; and
   (b) a departmental hat which illustrates the role of the department, and which is designed to protect the wearer from external pressures such as requests to do other jobs, extend your work role, take on other people's responsibilities, help others when you are already under pressure, and so forth.
2. Join other departments in the task of producing on at least two linked sheets of flip-chart paper a network of circles, each representing a department, and joined where appropriate by lines representing shared facilities, procedures, resources, and so on, as follows:

   - work objectives;
   - communications processes;
   - database;
   - IT systems;
   - standards of work performance;
   - reporting chain;
   - safety regulations;
   - operational processes/procedures;
   - equipment;
   - accommodation, parking, catering, etc;
   - conditions of work;
   - training and development; and
   - any other links.

   Include the departmental slogan within each circle on the flip-chart.
3. Take part in the presentation as explained by your trainer, describing your part in the network, your slogan, and what your hat is designed to protect you from.
4. Reconvene as a departmental team, and review your department's contribution to the network. Decide on *three* actions you can take to improve the effectiveness of the network. These will then be offered to the other departments on the workshop for their consideration.

Managing Boundaries

Summary
- Suitable for any number of participants.
- Teams complete an audit of the way they manage boundaries in terms of communication with other teams. They then seek ways of improving the management of these boundaries in the future.

Objectives   Communication, managing team boundaries, presentation, team leadership.

Materials
- Copies of the team briefing sheet.
- Copies of the audit sheet.
- Flip charts, paper and pens.

Timing   45–60 minutes.

Procedure
1. Individuals complete the audit for their current work team.
2. Teams collate the results and produce a summary of all responses.
3. Teams now consider areas of poorly managed boundaries and present an action plan for improving these.

Commentary   This can be an important activity in making team members aware of their links with other teams and influential individuals, and how they depend on them for continued success. It can also be used to focus on team leadership, and as a vehicle for individual development of the team leader.

Variations   None.

Team briefing: Managing Boundaries

At work, you and your team do not function in a vacuum, but have other teams and influential individuals around you. These teams and individuals need to be kept informed of what you and your team are doing, the resources you need, the changes being made, the publicity you require, deadlines, how they can help, the information and records you need from them, and so on.

Stage 1
Each individual in your team should complete the attached audit.

Stage 2
Collate the responses of each team member onto a flip chart, and consider the results.

Stage 3
Consider what actions you can take as a team to strengthen the communication with others who are important to you. Set out your plan on a flip chart, and select one member to present this plan to the other course participants.

Reproduced from *Team Development Games for Trainers* by Roderick R. Stuart, Gower, Aldershot

Individual audit: Managing Boundaries

Do you agree or disagree with the following statements? Our team:

Strongly agree	Agree	Statement	Disagree	Strongly disagree
....	....	1. Have an effective sponsor who acts on our behalf to gain support, publicity, access to resources.	....	....
....	....	2. Hold regular meetings with clients, customers, sponsors, users to discuss progress, issues, changes and so forth.	....	....
....	....	3. Keep our own functional managers fully informed on a regular basis.	....	....
....	....	4. Have a recognized and regular channel of communication to other teams.	....	....
....	....	5. Have an effective representation to other teams.	....	....
....	....	6. Always know what other teams need in terms of our support, resources, and so on.	....	....
....	....	7. Understand where our effort fits into that of other teams.	....	....
....	....	8. Can gain immediate access to other teams when necessary.	....	....
....	....	9. Receive regular feedback from other teams on the shared responsibilities.	....	....
....	....	10. Publicize our current progress and successes.	....	....
....	....	11. Share the recognition and credit with others where this is appropriate.	....	....

Reproduced from *Team Development Games for Trainers* by Roderick R. Stuart, Gower, Aldershot

Motive Power at Work

Summary
- Suitable for up to 20 participants.
- Individuals complete a motivation survey which includes various motivational factors affecting work relations. Teams then consolidate the views of individuals and arrive at a short list of factors which could be changed to increase motivation at work. Finally, the teams plan actions they can take which will lead to improved motivation within the team.

Objectives   Application, communication, diagnostic, team development.

Materials
- Copies of the briefing sheet.
- Copies of the survey sheet.
- Flip charts, paper and pens.

Timing   45–60 minutes.

Procedure
1. Explain the activity, and point out that the views of individuals will be confidential unless they themselves decide to share their views with others.
2. Hand out the instructions and the motivation survey to individuals and have these completed.
3. Form teams and complete the remainder of the activity.
4. Lead a discussion on the importance of motivation within the team and consider the actions each team has decided to implement.

Commentary   This motivation survey is not necessarily aligned to the various models of motivation such as those of Maslow, Herzberg, Vroom and others, but rather it considers the way individuals discuss their work in informal ways. Completion of this survey will certainly lead you back to the models of motivation should you wish. More importantly, however, it will enable you to facilitate change at work within teams. The completed team position can be used as a measure of current attitudes and progress over time.

Variations   None.

Briefing: Motive Power at Work

Part 1   Individual activity

Listed on the attached survey sheet are some of the factors people mention when they are discussing work and changes they would instigate to make life at work more satisfying.

Assume that you have twenty points to allocate to these factors. Divide these points amongst the factors in any way you wish, so that your completed checklist reflects what you would change in order to make your job more satisfactory from your personal point of view. If there are other factors that you feel particularly strongly about, add these to the survey list and score them. (At this stage, ignore the column marked team score.)

Part 2   Team activity

● First, transfer the scores of individuals who have completed the earlier survey list to a master sheet.

● Second, agree which are the most important six factors that would enable the team to become more effective, and then rank order these six factors, in descending order of importance.

● Third, decide on three positive actions you can take within the team that will increase the motivation of team members and which are achievable in the next three months.

● Fourth, select one person to report back to the group on the conclusions you have reached.

Reproduced from *Team Development Games for Trainers* by Roderick R. Stuart, Gower, Aldershot

Survey: Motive Power at Work

I would make sure that:

Factors	Your score	Team score
1. We discuss and find solutions to conflict within the team.	....	....
2. I know what I have to achieve and by when, and the quality of work expected of me.	....	....
3. When the priorities of work change, they are explained to me so that I understand the reasons for this change.	....	....
4. My work can be achieved with the resources I have or can readily obtain.	....	....
5. I am able to discuss difficulties without being seen as a whinger or uncooperative person.	....	....
6. There is less office politics and more co-operation.	....	....
7. I find the support I need when things go wrong.	....	....
8. People are treated fairly and openly.	....	....
9. Team members support and help each other when they face a workload peak.	....	....
10. Team members receive effective training.	....	....
11. I am not expected to do work for which I have not been trained.	....	....
12. Team members are not expected to cut corners on safety or health issues.	....	....
13. I am able to relax and be myself.	....	....
14. When I want to, I am able to work alone without interruptions from others.	....	....

Reproduced from *Team Development Games for Trainers* by Roderick R. Stuart, Gower, Aldershot

Factors	Your score	Team score
15. The information I receive is current, relevant, and helps me do my job.	....	....
16. I have a variety of work, which helps me to develop more skills for my future career development.	....	....
17. The management style is consistent throughout the team, department and so on.	....	....
18. I am accepted by others in the team for who I am, without having to pretend.	....	....
19. I am able to do my work in my own way and at my own speed, and that I make decisions where necessary	....	....
20. There is greater sensitivity to the feelings, attitudes and values of others.	....	....

Other factors:

Music Maestro

Summary
- Suitable for up to 20 participants.
- Teams compete to perform a tune they have selected, playing "instruments" they have created using any materials available to them in the training environment.

Objectives
Assertiveness, communication, creativity, decision making, influencing, planning, presentation, problem solving, team development.

Materials
- Copies of the team briefing sheet.
- Copies of the scoring sheet.

Timing
45–60 minutes.

Procedure
1. Form teams. If your objectives include leadership, decide if you need to nominate a new leader for each team, or expect a leader to "emerge".
2. Hand out the briefing sheets and ensure that they are understood by the teams.
3. Decide how performances will be scored, and by whom (if possible, select a panel of two to three judges). Use the judges as observers.
4. Let teams complete their planning and rehearsal stage.
5. Recall the teams, select the order of play, and complete the competition.
6. Return each team to their own location to review their own performance.
7. Lead a discussion to consolidate the learning points brought out by the game.

Commentary
This is naturally a noisy session, so you may care to warn others in the proximity! Groups should have a certain degree of openness, that is, should be relatively unreserved, communicative and constructive in their approach. The game would therefore be of limited value when used with groups which have just formed. You need complete commitment on the part of the teams for this activity to be successful. Also, the reflective stage may need to be extended to allow individuals to "settle down" after their performance.

Variations   Rather than let teams select their own tune, ask the group to agree on one tune. This is an additional constraint, and thus provides another opportunity for the trainer to experience and review the contributions of individuals.

Team briefing: Music Maestro

1. Using any materials which are present in the room, design musical instruments which can be used to play a tune selected by your group. Your team performance will be assessed at the end of the activity by a panel of judges, and points will be awarded for:

   (a) the number of different instruments used;
   (b) the quality of the sound; and
   (c) the length of time your team can play together and the panel recognize the tune being played.

   The marking system will be as follows:

   - 5 points per instrument.
   - 50 points "Top of the pops " down to 1 mark for "ugh".
   - 20 points for every ten seconds of recognizable music.

2. You have 25 minutes to complete your planning, brief the team, prepare instruments, and rehearse. At the end of that period you will be told where the musical contest will take place.
3. No member of the team is permitted to sing, whistle, or hum their tune.

Scoring sheet: Music Maestro

	Team A	Team B	Team C	Team D	Comments
Instruments (five points per instrument)	....	....	....	....	
Quality ("top of the pops" = 50 points, down to 1 point for "Ugh"	....	....	....	....	
Time (20 points for every ten seconds the tune is recognizable)	....	....	....	....	

Reproduced from *Team Development Games for Trainers* by Roderick R. Stuart, Gower, Aldershot

NewsClues

Summary
- Suitable for between 9 and 18 participants. Additional participants would be invited to be observers.
- Teams take part in a triangular competition to solve a puzzle concocted from a newspaper (see attached sheet of puzzle solutions) for which one of the other teams has the answer. Questions are taken in turn, and are restricted to those which elicit a straight "yes" or "no" response. The winning team is the one who lowers a flag and satisfies the trainer they have indeed solved their own puzzle.

Objectives   Assertiveness, communication, decision making, influencing, listening, problem solving, team development.

Materials
- Copies of the team briefing sheet.
- At least four copies of any daily newspaper of the same date.
- Copies of three puzzle solutions, each written on a separate sheet.
- Flip charts, paper and pens.

Timing   45–60 minutes.

Procedure
1. Form teams.
2. Hand out a copy of any daily newspaper to each team, plus the team briefing sheet, and one puzzle solution on a separate sheet.
3. Play the game, recording the time when each team put their flag down.
4. Teams return to a syndicate room to review their own performance against your suggested criteria.

Commentary   One of the advantages of this activity is that you as a trainer do not need to spend time in preparation. It provides a good opportunity to consider how teams operate together, how they need to be clear in formulating questions to elicit information and in recording responses, and how individuals can influence the team. The competitive aspect and its influence on individuals and teams can also be observed and reviewed.

Variations   Teams attempt to solve both their own and one opposing team puzzle (the team for which they do not have the solution!). In this case, the winning team is the one who solves both puzzles fastest.

116

Puzzle solutions: NewsClues

This sheet must be retained by the trainer. From it, the trainer selects one solution, which must be written on a separate sheet, to offer to each team. The fourth solution is simply to provide the trainer with a choice to offer to the teams.

1. The number of letters in the newspaper's title, and the dimensions in centimetres of the largest picture on the front page.
2. The first and last paragraphs of the opinion or leader page of the paper, written on a flip chart.
3. The first and final letters to the editor, read out to the course by a member of the team.
4. Timings of programmes from 4.00 p.m. to 6.00 p.m. on two TV channels.

Reproduced from *Team Development Games for Trainers* by Roderick R. Stuart, Gower, Aldershot

Team briefing: NewsClues

1. Your team are to take part in a triangular competition to find three different pieces of information in the newspapers you have been given. Each team has the solution to one puzzle that another team is trying to solve by asking the questions within the rules shown below. Hence you will have to ask another team whatever questions you think will lead your team to solve your own puzzle. The winning team is the one who lowers their flag first and then satisfies the course trainer that they have solved the puzzle. Teams who fail the trainer's scrutiny are automatically disqualified.
2. Before the first round of questions:

    (a) read the rules;
    (b) decide who will ask the questions in your team; and
    (c) make a flag or other signalling device which can be erected and then lowered when you finally want to offer your solution to the trainer.

Rules

1. Three teams play the game.
2. Each team is given the solution to one other team's puzzle (i.e. A has B's, B has C's, and C has A's).
3. A nominated person in each team can ask one question in turn to the team known to be holding their solution. Thus team A asks the first question, followed by team B, and then team C.
4. All questions except the final two must be closed questions (i.e. they must lead to an answer of yes-no, true-false, correct-incorrect or other similar either-or response).
5. Teams must give responsible, considered and accurate answers as far as possible to all questions, limiting each answer to the information requested.
6. The winner is the team who can accurately solve their puzzle quickest. They signify their readiness to solve the puzzle by lowering their flag, after which they cannot ask further questions. This time is recorded by the trainer.
7. The trainer is the sole arbiter of the accuracy of the solution.

Newspaper Chase

Summary
- Suitable for up to 20 participants.
- Team leaders select their own level of complexity in the completion of a standard task. The competitive task is to interpret information given to the teams and solve a puzzle in a daily newspaper. Those who choose a higher level of complexity are given additional impositions on their time.

Objectives
Communication, conflict management, delegation, influencing, problem solving, team development, team leadership, time management.

Materials
- One copy of *The Daily Telegraph* of the same date for each team taking part.
- One copy of the solution sheet for the trainer.
- Copies of the team briefing.
- Sufficient copies of the team information packs to allow one set of information strips for each team.
- Flip charts, paper and pens.

Timing
45–60 minutes.

Procedure

1. Before the game, print and cut up into their constituent strips of information (numbered from 1 to 32) sufficient copies of the team information pack to allow one full set of strips for each team.
2. Form teams and nominate a leader for each. (You may also wish to appoint one observer per team.)
3. Hand out the team briefing and ensure that the teams understand the complexity levels. Team leaders decide which level to go for.
4. For each team opting for *Level Two* and *Three*, extract three *different* pieces of information from each pack. You retain the three pieces for *Level Two* teams, but give the three pieces for each *Level Three* team to another team. Tell each *Level Three* which team has their missing information and that they must negotiate with them to obtain the missing information. *Level Two* teams must negotiate directly with you for their missing information, which you will give them providing they ask the right questions.
5. If you wish to highlight convergent–divergent thinking processes, introduce the additional task of creating a suitable piece of head-

gear out of their newspapers. Give teams 10 minutes to decide together on the criteria they would use to judge a creative piece of headgear.

6. Play the game. Remember to take leaders out of teams who have opted for *Level Two* and *Level Three*. *Level Two* leaders are called out once; *Level Three* leaders are called out twice. Do this at your own discretion, once the game is under way. When they are out of the team rooms on these call-outs, the team leaders have no specific role or task to carry out.

7. Teams review their performance against the criteria or check lists you draw up.

Commentary This is an excellent leadership development game, which benefits from having a second trainer to manage the team negotiations for *Level Three* teams and hand out information as necessary to *Level Two* teams. The strict time limit leads to greater stress on the leader and consequent changes in behaviour. Convergent–divergent thinking processes can be explored since there is an example of each in the game.

Variations None.

Team briefing: Newspaper Chase

You have 40 minutes from the time stated in which to complete your task – unless there is contrary information within your pack! You should make a decision now with regard to the level of complexity you will aim to achieve (see the description below for details).

Task
Your task is to analyse the information you will be given in an information pack and arrive at the correct solution. (There may be a second task, to create an original piece of headgear. If so, your trainer will confirm this second task to you.)

Complexity levels
There are three levels of complexity to the task, which broadly relate to the levels of leadership we would expect in this group, as follows:

- *Level One* is for nominated leaders who think they are inexperienced, and for this level, all the information will be given to the leader. He or she will not be interrupted, but will be left to lead as necessary.
- *Level Two* is for those leaders who think they are relatively experienced. If you select this level, some information will be missing from your pack. You will have to decide and then explain to the trainer what you want, and he or she will give you this information, providing you ask the right questions. During the activity your leader may be called out of the room for a period of 2 minutes.
- *Level Three* is for those who relish a challenge. Some information will be missing from your pack and the tutor will tell you who has that information. You will then have to negotiate with them to obtain this necessary information. Also, the leader may be called out of the room for two separate periods of time of 2 minutes each. This may happen at any time during the activity

The nominated leader of each team must make the decision on which level of complexity to go for, after consulting with his or her team members when the team briefings are first handed out. There are no prizes for achieving any particular level of complexity – only the satisfaction of completing the game successfully and the learning points that you will gain in the process.

Reproduced from *Team Development Games for Trainers* by Roderick R. Stuart, Gower, Aldershot

Solution: Newspaper Chase

This single sheet is to be retained by the trainer.

Statement
The statement which provides the first part of the solution is the weather forecast for your particular region. It should be written exactly as it appears in *The Daily Telegraph*, including the capitals and lower-case words where necessary.

Cost of space
The cost of the space (which measures 3 columns across, by 4.75 inches down) is calculated as follows:

● 14 lines per column inch at £8. 16s. 6d. (£8.825) per line = £123.55 (£123. 11s. 0d.) per column inch
● There are 4.75 column inches in each column = £123.55 × 4.75 = £586.86 (£586. 17s. 2d.) per column
● There are 3 columns across the page = £586.86 × 3 = £1,760.58 (£1,760. 11s. 7d.)

Hence the total cost in pre-decimal currency of the space taken up by the weather forecast section on the back page of *The Daily Telegraph* is:

£1,760. 11s. 7d.

Reproduced from *Team Development Games for Trainers* by Roderick R. Stuart, Gower, Aldershot

Team information pack: Newspaper Chase

1. The piece of printing you are searching for can be located on the final page of the newspaper.

2. The piece of printing you are looking for is contained in the final three columns of print.

3. The piece of printing you are looking for changes every day.

4. The piece of printing you are looking for is in the bottom half of the page.

5. The piece of printing you are looking for concerns the climate.

6. The piece of printing you are looking for covers that part of the country in which this course is taking place.

7. In addition to the piece of printing we want you to quote, you are asked to give us the total cost of the entire section of the newspaper within which that piece of printing can be found.

8. Your statement may help delegates on this course should they be travelling during the next day or so.

9. Your costing should include all lines which *could* be printed inside the boxes which surround the section of printing you will be studying.

10. Newspaper charges are as follows (as at 1 January 1997): personal (private) £8 1s 0d per line; charity appeals £6 11s 2d per line; traders £8 16s 6d per line.

11. This part of the newspaper is costed at the trader rate.

12. It is possible to insert fourteen lines of print into any one column inch of the paper.

13. Your final cost for the section must be calculated in pre-decimal currency.

Reproduced from *Team Development Games for Trainers* by Roderick R. Stuart, Gower, Aldershot

14. The complete section of printing you will be studying is 4.75 inches in depth.

15. In pre-decimal currency, there were 240 pennies in £1.

16. Your solution must be given to us by a particular individual who has been chosen because he or she fits a set of criteria which is included in this information pack.

17. Use these criteria to rank order members of your team: oldest = 1, youngest = highest number; smallest = 1, tallest = highest number; Born furthest away from London = 1, born nearest to London = highest number.

18. During the summer months, you may find information of value to sufferers from hay fever in the section of printing you are considering.

19. The newspaper was established in 1855 and has covered your particular section since the early 1920s when the Met Office was established.

20. The newspaper usually has 32 pages and your information is found in the same place each day.

21. The information contained in your section would be of interest to farmers.

22. Many car drivers would be interested in the information provided in the section you are going to cost for us.

23. If you have been tasked with creating a piece of headgear from the newspaper, do not use the front or back sheets in the hat construction.

24. If you have been tasked with creating a piece of headgear from the newspaper, you have an additional 10 minutes to do this. This gives a total of 50 minutes for the completed task.

25. The section of the newspaper you need is also included on the front page.

26. Your solution must be given to us by a specific individual. He or she will be the person with the highest final ranking order, having added together a number of different placings.

27. Part of the solution we want from you is a statement which would be written down, using the exact wording as it appears, in capitals and lower-case print.

28. Another newspaper uses Page Three in a different way to your newspaper, but the title of that paper may give you a clue to what it is you are looking for today.

29. The costed solution must be offered to your trainer within 40 minutes of the start of the activity.

30. If you look at the Letters to the Editor, you may find letters discussing the subject you are seeking. Over the years more letters have been published on this topic than on any other concern of readers.

31. To find out the rank order of your team, add up the number of places each person has in the criteria you are using. (e.g. 1st, 2nd, 3rd: therefore, the total in this example is 6). The lowest total is the highest rank in the order.

Reproduced from *Team Development Games for Trainers* by Roderick R. Stuart, Gower, Aldershot

Noah's Lark

Summary
- Suitable for any number of participants.
- Teams compete to construct a diagram (described in the game as a scalar) to show how ten animals on Noah's Ark are uniquely different. The diagram builds up using pictures of the animals, as teams decide where to place the animals. The game involves selecting a game strategy, purchase of information, and working against time to achieve a result.

Objectives

Assertiveness, communication, conflict management, decision making, influencing, planning, team development, team leadership, time management.

Materials
- One copy of the printed master scalar to be held by the trainer.
- Copies of team briefing sheet.
- Copies of information description sheet.
- Copies of additional information sheet.
- Copies of scalar example (Item T).
- Copies of the complete set of descriptions and illustrations of animals (*Note:* each team will require 5 complete sets).
- Flip charts, paper and pens.
- Each team will require a separate room in which, first, to discuss strategy privately, and secondly, to set out their patterns of illustrations on desks or floor.

Timing

90–120 minutes.

Procedure

1. Prior to the game, print out sets of the information that teams can purchase (sufficient for one set per team). If teams come to you to purchase information, cut off the appropriate item from their set, give it to the team representative, and record the purchase.
2. Form teams and select leaders and observers.
3. Introduce the game as an opportunity to rehearse the skills being developed. Explain that they will need to assimilate and use a great deal of information, and that the game can increase tension as well as satisfaction!
4. Hand out the various materials and send teams to their rooms.

5. Play the game to a conclusion. Agree points totals per team, and announce the "winners".
6. Review the game briefly before sending each team to a private location to complete their team review. This should concentrate on your stated objectives.
7. Lead a discussion regarding the similarities between this activity and participants' work context, and how they can learn from the game to become more effective at work.

Commentary   This is an excellent game which requires you to be in complete control of both the information and progress of the activity. Two trainers are better here than one! Practical, intellectual, individual and team activity as well as emotional involvement are present in the completion of the scalar, offering opportunities for individual and team review processes. Using video would be valuable for the review stages, providing that personal integrity is maintained and the review concentrates on "what happened" rather than the individuals involved.

Variations   This game uses the classification methodology adopted to differentiate fungi. Hence, simply by selecting ten fungi, it is possible to design a variation using the same stages. Other variations would be to use the attributes of cars, houses, clothing, or any manufactured products to design an "in-house" version. Such a custom-built variation could be of value in other training programmes. Teams could be required to design their version of the game, establishing their own attributes, levels of scalar, and so forth.

Team briefing: Noah's Lark

1. The purpose of this game is to classify ten animals. Each animal must appear on your diagram (scalar) as a unique sub-species, which can be identified as being different from all the remaining animals.

2. Your completed scalar must agree with the printed master scalar, which is held by the trainer.

3. To assist you, there are descriptions of each of the ten animals involved. Some of this information is not essential!

4. In addition, you can decide as a team to "purchase" further information. A brief description of each item of information available is shown on the attached list, together with its cost to you in points. If you decide to purchase information, send a member of your team to the trainer with details of your requirement. The trainer will then give you the appropriate item of information in writing. Be warned that success is very unlikely if you purchase no information!

5. The team which invests in the information with the highest payoff (to suit their particular strengths and strategy) will be the most successful.

6. *Points* Teams begin the game with 800 points, which decrease with time and the cost of any information purchased. Details are set out below and on the information sheet.

7. *Time limits* To gain any points, you must complete the scalar in under 40 minutes, from the time you are told to start. Within this time frame, each minute taken costs 20 points.

8. *Bonus points* If you announce a "target time" before the activity begins (this states the maximum time you will take to complete and hand in your solution) and achieve the task within that target, your team score a bonus equal to the number of time points you are left with (e.g. if you declare and achieve a time of 12 minutes, your remaining time points would total 560, *plus* 560 bonus points giving a grand total of 1120 points).

9. If, however, you do not achieve the target time, you forfeit points on a sliding scale, that is, you lose 10 points for being 1 minute over target, and this loss *doubles* for each further minute you are over target (20 points for 2 minutes, 40 points for 3 minutes, 80 points for 4 minutes, and so on).

10. *Consultant* You may decide to use the services of a consultant. He or she will advise you, using his or her experience of similar previous projects – not necessarily exactly the same! If you do decide to use the consultant, this consultation costs 150 points for a 2-minute session, provided that you book the consultant within the first 5 minutes of the game. This booking can be for any time not already booked by other teams. If you call the consultant in without booking him or her first, the consultation will cost 200 points.

Additional information: Noah's Lark

These items of information are retained by the trainer, and can be purchased by teams.

Item	Information
A	Edible animals would appear on your scalar above the attribute indicating *docile* ⇔ *aggressive*.
B	In all, there are more than three levels in the scalar from top to bottom, which includes the title.
C	The weight of each animal would appear below the horns level.
D	Edible animals would appear to the left of non-edible animals.
E	*docile* ⇔ *aggressive* is relatively unimportant, although it is used to classify the animals.
F	The coldest animal would appear to the right of the scale for each sub-category. However, this information may be of marginal value to you.
G	Whether or not the animal has horns is a very important level in the scalar.
H	One of the attributes used is *weight*. Animals over 30 lb are placed on the left of the dichotomy.
I	The presence of a distinct smell is a characteristic which is *not* important.
J	Whether or not the animal is *edible* is of importance.
K	One of the attributes used is *Lives on land* ⇔ *Not so*. Animals living on land appear on the left-hand side of this dichotomy.

Reproduced from *Team Development Games for Trainers* by Roderick R. Stuart, Gower, Aldershot

Item	Information
L	*aggressive ⇔ docile* is an attribute which is used within the scalar.
M	Animals are classified by *size*, using the measurement of the smallest likely specimen. Where the smallest likely specimen is greater than 30 lbs, that animal would appear on the left-hand side of the dichotomous variable.
N	The first level of the scalar is *horns ⇔ no horns*.
O	The terms used in this activity have been defined as follows: ● *Attributes* A general description which can be applied to *all* animals in the scalar (e.g. weight, edible, horns). Each level of the scalar shows a different attribute. ● *Characteristic* A characteristic indicates the *presence or absence* of an attribute on a particular animal, such as horns, size, weight, where the animal lives, and so forth (e.g. a bat has no horns). ● *Sub-species* A unique animal, which has its own set of characteristics and which can be distinguished from all other sub-species. ● *Scalar* A diagram showing a number of levels of attributes. ● *Dichotomy* The division of an attribute into two groups. One group has the particular attribute, whilst the other does not. For example, if the attribute was *land living animals*, the division would be: *lives on land ⇔ does not live on land* *Note:* these definitions may not agree with those found in a dictionary!
P	Any reference to the following information would not be used in this particular classification: ● Smell ● Food eaten ● Breeding habits ● Colour ● Friendliness to children ● Geographic area of origin ● Location on the Ark ● Future use of animal

Reproduced from *Team Development Games for Trainers* by Roderick R. Stuart, Gower, Aldershot

Item	Information
Q	The attributes used in this scalar (from top to bottom on the scalar) are as follows: • *horns ⟺ no horns* • *weight over 30 lb ⟺ weight under 30 lb* • *lives on land ⟺ does not live on land* • *edible ⟺ not edible* • *docile ⟺ aggressive*

Reproduced from *Team Development Games for Trainers* by Roderick R. Stuart, Gower, Aldershot

Description of information available: Noah's Lark

The following items of information can be purchased by teams from the trainer at the cost in points as stated against each item.

Item	Points cost	Information: broad descriptions
A	5	Information indicating the relative position of two attributes.
B	5	Information indicating the possible number of levels in the scalar.
C	5	Information showing relative position of two attributes on the scalar.
D	5	Information about the position of one characteristic on the scalar.
E	5	Information about a particular attribute.
F	5	Information indicating the relative position of one of the characteristics.
G	10	Information about a particular attribute.
H	10	Information indicating the use of a characteristic, and its relative position.
I	15	Information about a particular characteristic.
J	20	Information about a particular characteristic.
K	30	Information about one of the attributes used.
L	30	Information about one of the attributes used

Reproduced from *Team Development Games for Trainers* by Roderick R. Stuart, Gower, Aldershot

Item	Points cost	Information: broad descriptions
M	40	Information describing a scale of measurement using one attribute.
N	40	Information on the first level of the scalar.
O	100	Descriptions of all terms used in the scalar.
P	100	Information you have which is not used in the scalar.
Q	150	Information concerning the major attributes used, and their relative position on the scalar.
R	150	The first level of the scalar.
S	75	The last level of the scalar.
T	225	An example of a completed scalar, but for fungi.

An example of a completed scalar (Item T): Noah's Lark

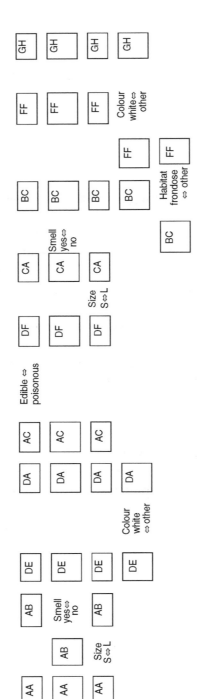

Note: The abbreviations (AA etc.) stand for the individual names of fungi.

Reproduced from *Team Development Games for Trainers* by Roderick R. Stuart, Gower, Aldershot

The first level of the scalar (Item R): Noah's Lark

| Hill Goat | Pie Goat | Oxen | Sea Lion | | Cock Bird | Horn Toad | Horn Fish | ⇐Horns No Horns⇒ | | Monkey | Bat | Fish |

The last level of the scalar (Item S): Noah's Lark

| Pie Goat | ⇐Docile not docile⇒ | Oxen | | Horn Toad | ⇐Docile not docile⇒ | Horn Fish |

Reproduced from *Team Development Games for Trainers* by Roderick R. Stuart, Gower, Aldershot

Illustrations and descriptions of the animals: Noah's Lark

Pie Goat This sensitive looking beast weighs in at around 65 lbs, and is as tough as old boots. Noah uses part of the hide as moccasins and the rest of the hide as a bumper for the boat. He has tried to eat parts of the goat, and blames this episode on his taking 100 years to build the ark! Now the pie goat is definitely not on the menu. Like the hill goat, it is docile.	
Cock Bird The most endearing quality of this bird is its ability to wake Noah every morning, including Sunday. This infuriates Noah, since he is some few hundred years ahead of the coming of the Lord and does not keep the Sabbath. However, the cock bird makes a pretty picture – and a glorious Sunday lunch, producing a weight of about 8 lbs when plucked.	
Monkey Noah uses this 40 lb chunk of galvanized lightning to shin up the mast every so often and spot land ahead. Again, he has found from bitter experience that the monkey is not edible, but can be made to play party tricks. It comes from North Africa, and Noah understands it wants to be dropped off from his Ark around Gibraltar. Its behaviour makes Noah think it could become a tourist attraction, being friendly and easy to picture with children.	

Reproduced from *Team Development Games for Trainers* by Roderick R. Stuart, Gower, Aldershot

Sea Trout

This Scottish sea trout provides Noah with some delicious meals, weighing up to 2 lb on average. It is intelligent, quick witted, and an admirable travelling companion. It has an unusually fishy smell, but no other unpleasant habits.

Ox

This 150 lb sleeping barn door is most useful as a plug in the side of the Ark, since it helps to keep those animals in which should be in, and those out which should be out. It cannot be eaten, but Noah thinks it may be useful at some time in the future for ploughing. As soon as the plough is invented he will try out this theory. One problem will be that the ox is very aggressive toward strangers – including Noah.

Hill Goat

The hill goat is most easily recognized because it smells! A mixture of rotting old socks, stale cabbage water, and the fragrance of rancid goat's milk sums up this delightful animal. It weighs in at about 45 lb, much of which is rain-soaked wool and cracked horns. It feeds on just about any piece of rubbish Noah throws out. In spite of this, it is edible, and considered a delicacy! Noah finds it docile, as well as carrying fleas by the bucketful.

Reproduced from *Team Development Games for Trainers* by Roderick R. Stuart, Gower, Aldershot

Horn Fish

This sensitive little fish has an endearing habit of sneaking up on slumbering guppies and frightening the daylights out of them. Fortunately, it only weighs 3 lb, and takes up little room under the boat. Noah has tried eating it, but even with cajun batter it tastes foul. It shoals in the North African section of the Med, spawning in the upper reaches of the Tunisian Groboh river, where it is known for its undesirable aggressive tendencies.

Horn Toad

Noah often wonders why he took the trouble to rescue this slimy creature. Living under water, with its head occasionally breaking the surface, it weighs about 8 lb and looks like one of Noah's relatives. He has no knowledge of its breeding habits, and does not wish to find out, in spite of its somewhat docile manner. Equally, it is poisonous, as Noah found out when he dined with some prominent dignitaries who promptly died on him.

Sea Lion

Noah thinks this sea-loving creature has a future – either as part of a Disney World show or as added horse power for the Ark, since it spends all of its time under the boat in the sea. It weighs around 200 lb when sober, and slightly less when inebriated (Noah being the drunk). This creature is not edible! Noah finds it amusing that the sea lion refers to its 'horns' as 'tusks' – a tribal word meaning 'to hang down'.

Reproduced from *Team Development Games for Trainers* by Roderick R. Stuart, Gower, Aldershot

Bat

Noah has included this fruit bat because it only weighs a few ounces and hangs around all day looking stupid. He has an idea that it may have a hearing problem and is blind, and so he is interested in finding out how it manages to fly round the mast of the Ark catching flies. One day he hopes to trace the colony back to Greece, from which they were ejected for fighting with other bats. It has the same nutritional value as a carpet slipper, so is not deemed to be edible.

Reproduced from *Team Development Games for Trainers* by Roderick R. Stuart, Gower, Aldershot

Printed master scalar: Noah's Lark

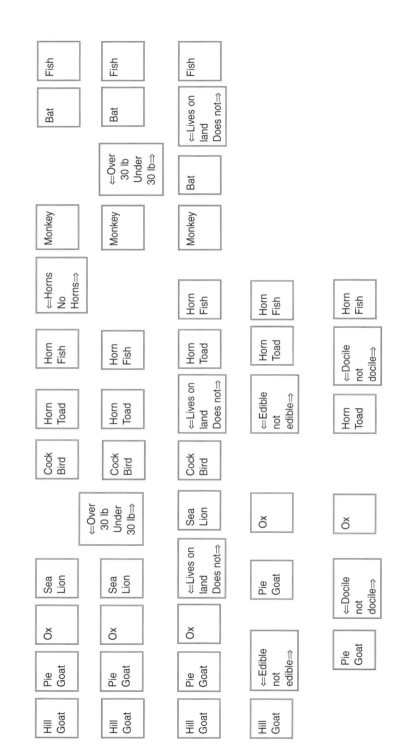

Noughts and Crosses

Summary
- Suitable for up to 12 participants. Additional participants would observe.
- Teams play noughts and crosses for an incentive such as free time during the course. One individual in each team is selected to call out the next move to the trainer who inserts the nought or cross on a flip-chart-sized board.

Objectives Assertiveness, communication, decision making, influencing, listening.

Materials
- Copies of rules.
- Template for playing board.
- Flip charts and pens (or overhead projector).

Timing 20–30 minutes.

Procedure
1. Beforehand, prepare playing boards, either on flip charts or on an overhead projector, to allow two games of noughts and crosses to be played simultaneously as shown on the attached template.
2. Explain that the group are going to play noughts and crosses for an incentive such as free time during the course. There is a scale of reward and a basic set of rules, a copy of which is given to the teams.
3. Teams are formed, who each select their own caller.
4. The first games of noughts and crosses are played. The two opposing teams play two games simultaneously against each other, as shown on the template. The scores are then reviewed. Teams are given a short time to discuss privately how they can improve their score next time.
5. The next sequence of games is played. This sequence should result in both teams gaining maximum scores, since they usually realize that by collaborating, a win–win situation results.

Commentary This short game is excellent for highlighting the interdependent nature of teams, and the fact that they can gain more by collaborating than by competing. You can follow on from this to consider work situations which are similar, and for which teams can plan actions that they could take to eliminate wasteful competition.

Variations None.

Rules: Noughts and Crosses

1. The games are played for free time during the course. For each line your team win, you will be given 5 minutes of free time. For each nought or cross in the corresponding square in *both* matrices (e.g. A1 and X7), you will be given 1 minute of free time. If you end up with fewer than four winning lines, you pay a penalty of 20 minutes' extra training.
2. Your team must nominate one person to call out your agreed next move. As an example, the caller could say 'A1' or 'X7'.
3. The call must be made within five seconds of the other team's call. Failure to respond within the time limit means that your team forfeit that move.
4. Two games are to be played simultaneously by the two teams on this board (to be indicated by the trainer).

Template: Noughts and Crosses

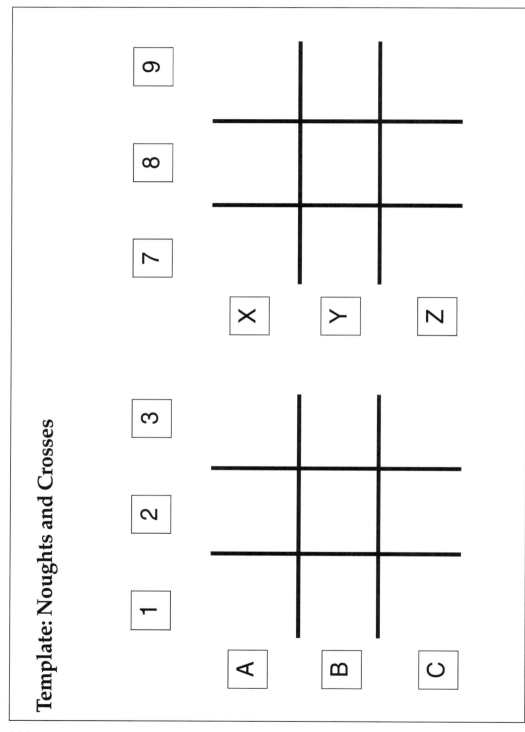

On Average ...

Summary
- Suitable for any number of participants.
- Teams are formed at random. They then exchange individual members of the team until they have arrived at the average weight of the group, within a stated time frame. The activity can be made competitive.

Objectives   Assertiveness, communication, influencing.

Materials
- Copies of the team briefing.
- Paper and pens.

Timing   20 minutes.

Procedure
1. Explain that the purpose of the activity is to find a team whose average weight is the same as the course average.
2. Set a strict time limit by which the teams must announce their solutions.
3. Ask each person in the whole group to state their weight. Add weights together, divide by the number in the group to establish the mean average weight.
4. Form teams by some random process (e.g. alphabetic name order, age, chair sequence).
5. Teams establish their own average weight, and then negotiate the exchange of individual members with other teams to reach a final average team weight that is as close as possible to the average group weight within the time limit.

Commentary   This is an excellent short game as an introductory session, especially when the participants on the course know each other, and when you want to find a novel way of forming subsequent teams who will stay together for some time. A clear time limit has to be set, and teams must be encouraged to use all of the time available to reach their objective.

Variations   Instead of weight, you could use other criteria, such as age, date in the month of birth, distance travelled to the course, or the first two digits of car licence plates.

Team briefing: On Average ...

Let us assume, say, that 50 per cent of this group are under the average weight of the group, while the other 50 per cent are over that average weight.

In this game, you are asked to negotiate a team whose average weight will be as close as possible to the average weight of the whole group. The team with the average weight closest to the course average will be the winning team.

Stage 1
Record the weights of all course members. Find the average weight of the whole group.

Stage 2
Form small teams at random (team numbers to be decided by the trainer). You now have 3 minutes in which to decide your team strategy.

Stage 3
By exchanging members with other teams, make the average weight of your team equal to the average weight of the whole course. Follow your agreed team strategy, collect information from other teams, and then negotiate exchanges of team members. Only one member of your team may be away at a time, and you may receive only one visitor at a time.

You have 20 minutes in which to complete the whole activity.

Reproduced from *Team Development Games for Trainers* by Roderick R. Stuart, Gower, Aldershot

Open Access

Summary
- Suitable for any number of participants.
- Teams complete a survey of their present training location to establish how easy it would be for disabled students to use the facilities as a learning environment. The teams use the appropriate official notes on access for disabled persons.

Objectives
Communication, decision making, delegation, feedback, planning, presentation, team development, team leadership.

Materials
- Copies of the team briefing sheet.
- Copies of Design Note 18, produced by the Department of Education & Science, Architects & Buildings Group, and available from:
  Publications Despatch Centre,
  Department of Education and Employment,
  Government Building,
  Honeypot Lane, Stanmore,
  Middlesex HA7 1AZ
  (*Note:* Although provision of this item is preferable, it is not essential for the course. You can use your own organizational quality standards for access instead.)
- Copies of the "Team leadership development" check list (see pp. 256–257).
- Flip charts, paper and pens.

Timing
45–60 minutes.

Procedure
1. Explain the purpose of the activity (which will reflect the objectives you want to achieve).
2. Form teams, and then select team leaders and observers for each team. If you wish to use observers, these should be selected at the same time as the teams.
3. Hand out the team briefing sheets and ask the leaders to organize the completion of the various tasks to be achieved.
4. Complete the activity.
5. Ask teams to make their presentations, which should be limited to 5 minutes per team.

6. Observers offer feedback to the leaders. This can be done with all leaders present. Working within their teams, team members complete the "Team leadership development" checklist at the same time.

7. Teams review their own performance including that of the team leader.

8. Lead a discussion which reviews the effectiveness of the teams, and considers how they can promote access to learning/working facilities in their own work environment for people who are disabled. Also, analyse the team presentation in terms of how the team planned and worked together, and assess the overall effectiveness of their communicated message.

Commentary This is a good activity as a team leadership development activity where physical strength is not a prerequisite of success. There are also elements of realism and relevance to the work environment, which often result in individuals taking positive action on return to work. The design sheets are comprehensive and the information falls into convenient categories to aid the planning and breakdown of work. The activity is also useful if you are developing teams through well-planned and coherent presentations in which all team members must make some contribution. Generally, I have found that teams, given the chance, tend to waste time in aimless discussion, rather than focus on the preparation of a structured plan. Limit the amount of time for the survey stage to about 70 per cent of the total time available, and this will bring dividends in the quality of teamwork in the presentations.

Variations Where it is not possible to obtain the government-approved design notes, you can instead use your own organizational quality standards for access in order to carry out this activity.

Team briefing: Open Access

Your organization has made a policy decision that the location which you are at present occupying must be made completely accessible to disabled people living in the community. It has been acknowledged that the product or service provided is used by many disabled people, who have extreme difficulty in seeing that product or service and making purchasing choices. This location has been chosen as a site through which you intend to learn the special needs of disabled people, and change the product or service to enable them to use it with greater ease and comfort.

To make the location accessible, you have been asked to consider the attached design sheets, and make recommendations. Teams have a number of factors to examine within the time available, at the end of which all teams present their findings to the group.

Each member of your team is expected to take an active part in and make a contribution to the team's final presentation.

Reproduced from *Team Development Games for Trainers* by Roderick R. Stuart, Gower, Aldershot

Pegging Away

Summary
- Suitable for 5 to 7 participants at any one time: that is, for each iteration of the activity (see notes under Commentary below).
- A team is asked to mark out an area of ground with string and pegs, and some geometric knowledge (although they are not told of the geometric knowledge requirement). In addition, they must be able to identify a point 5 metres from ground level.

Objectives   Communication, delegation, team development, team leadership.

Materials
- One copy of the trainer's notes.
- One copy of the team briefing sheet.
- One ball of parcel string (50 m).
- Six pegs (tent pegs are ideal).
- One mallet.
- One 1.5 m length of wood.

Timing   45–60 minutes.

Procedure
1. In advance of the game, choose a clear site that is fairly flat and has a suitable tree, telephone pole or wall available.
2. Select observers for the process review stage, who should observe stages 3, 4, and 5. With 7 participants, use two as observers; with 5–6 participants, use 1 as an observer.
3. Form teams, and select a leader for each team. Brief him or her on the task, and the leader will then brief the team.
4. Run the game.
5. Ask the observers to review what took place. Teams and individuals can also review their performance.
6. Lead a short discussion which considers the lessons learned from the activity in relation to the work environment of participants.

Commentary   This game can be run as one of a series of concurrent activities where teams move from one activity to the next, with a different leader in charge for each activity. It becomes competitive when you time the completion by each team.

It is an excellent game to highlight interdependence within teams, where people's differing skills and knowledge complement each other. Teams arrive at creative solutions (e.g. using a torch beam to determine the required height), and these can be reviewed accordingly.

Variations   The game can also be staged indoors, by scaling down the measurements considerably, and using a ruler, blue tack or pins, and string. Because the teams are then in a confined space, their approach is different, becoming more static and analytical, rather than active and experimental.

Trainer's notes: Pegging Away

This game requires a knowledge of geometry (similar triangles, and Pythagoras' theorem). If the team leader does not recognize this, then he or she either has to have someone in the team who does (e.g. a carpenter who knows the 3: 4: 5 rule), or must be told to remember: In a right-angled triangle, the square on the hypotenuse is equal to the sum of the squares of the other two sides. Thus for a right-angled triangle with sides of 3 m and 4 m, the hypotenuse will be 5 m (the same is true of any multiple of 3:4:5). In our example in Figure 1, therefore the diagonal of the kite shape will be 10 m.

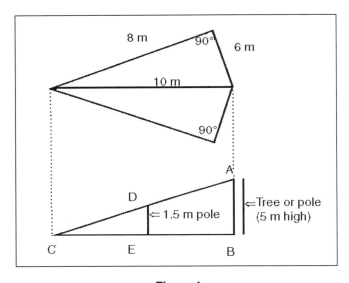

Figure 1

If we now turn to the properties of similar triangles, we will see that the ratios of the sides of the two triangles in Figure 1 are the same, as follows:

$$\frac{AB}{BC} = \frac{DE}{EC}$$

i.e. $\quad \frac{5}{10} = \frac{1.5}{3}$

Hence, by moving the 1.5 m pole in 3 m from C, then by lying on the ground at point C and looking up through the top of the pole towards the tree (or shining a torch beam up along the same trajectory), a point 5 m up the tree can be fixed.

Reproduced from Team Development Games for Trainers by Roderick R. Stuart, Gower, Aldershot

Team briefing: Pegging Away

Note: This briefing is to be read to the leader by the trainer, and then retained by the trainer.

Specialist radio equipment will arrive in about 35 minutes from now. It will be assembled by engineers, and must be operational one hour from now.

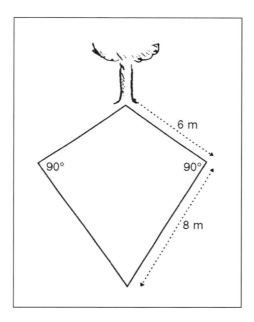

Figure 2

The equipment will require a flat surface in the shape of a kite as shown on the drawing (see Figure 2). As you can see, the kite has to be marked out from a tree on which engineers will want to install an antenna at a height of 5 metres.

Your team task is to set out the kite shape accurately, and to be able to point to the 5 metres height up this tree. You can only use the equipment in front of you as follows:

- one ball of string (50 m);
- one mallet;
- six pegs; and;
- one pole measuring 1.5 m.

You have 30 minutes to complete the task, starting now.

Reproduced from *Team Development Games for Trainers* by Roderick R. Stuart, Gower, Aldershot

Penny Pitcher

Summary
- Suitable for any number of participants.
- Teams select and train their pitcher, and then observe as he or she attempts to toss thirty coins into a 1 metre square. The winning team is the one which gets the greatest number of their coins inside the square.

Objectives   Application, assertiveness, communication, delegation, feedback, team development, team leadership.

Materials
- Copies of the team briefing sheet.
- Copies of the team review sheet.
- Sufficient large-sized coins for all teams to have at least 30. (The value of the coins is not important – except insofar as the winning team are allowed to keep all the coins.)
- Sticky tape for making the 1 metre square and the pitching line.
- Paper and pens.

Timing   60–90 minutes.

Procedure
1. Form teams, but do not appoint team leaders. (However, if your objectives include leadership or assertiveness development, see Variations below. In the variation, you will see that you are required to appoint team leaders some 2–4 hours prior to the game.)
2. Explain the game and hand out the team briefing sheet.
3. Mark out an area 1 metre square with the sticky tape, and also a pitching line about 3 metres from the leading edge of the square.
4. Play the game.
5. Let teams review their own performance against the criteria set out in the team review sheet you will hand out. This will include relating team performance in this activity to their work situation, and using as many of the check lists as necessary (see pp. 256–267).

Commentary   This game enables you to explore and develop a number of personal skills used within teams, as well as to further the general development of the team. It can also be applied to the way teams operate at work, by considering the review sheet and relevant check lists.

Variations   Some time before the game (2–4 hours) , nominate a team leader whose task is to ensure that his or her team wins the competition. He or she delegates the task of pitcher to a member of the team, then monitors the pitcher's performance during the game and changes the pitcher if necessary. Feedback can then be offered on their leadership performance, and in particular, on their skills of delegation. You may also consider using this activity to rehearse assertiveness skills by agreeing with a passive person that he or she should adopt the leadership role.

Team briefing: Penny Pitcher

In this competitive game we want you to train and then observe a member of your team pitching coins into a specified area to win a competition. The winning team will keep all the money!

Ground rules

● One member of the team must be nominated as the team pitcher.
● He or she must pitch at least 5 times before the team can ask for a "stand back" to discuss their position and change the pitcher if necessary.
● The winning team will be the team which pitches most coins inside the area marked with sticky tape.
● The trainer is the sole arbiter, and his or her decision is final.
● Each team has a total of 30 coins to pitch. Once pitched, a coin may not be touched again by any of the team members, and all members must remain behind the pitching line.

Stage 1
Working as a team, select and train one member who is capable of pitching a coin at least 3 metres, so that it lands within a 1 metre square. (The trainer will show you where the pitching area is to be.)

Stage 2
Take part in the competition.

Stage 3
Still working as a team, review your team's performance as directed by the trainer.

Team review: Penny Pitcher

In the review of your team performance, concentrate on the following specific points:

- How you discussed the job of the pitcher, what skills were needed, and so on.
- What information and any other data or advice you may have used.
- How you selected the pitcher.
- How was he or she trained.
- Who decided he or she was your best option as a 'trained' pitcher.
- How you selected a back-up pitcher.
- How you planned to change the pitcher (or continue with the first).
- What you might do differently in a re-run of this activity, or in other similar competitions.
- How the team coped with success or failure.

Application to work
Having carried out the review of your team performance in this activity, the final stage is to link the team performance to your work situation. Working as a team, draw as many links and parallels as you can between what happened in the game and your work practices involved in selecting, training and inducting people into your teams, setting work objectives, measuring performance and rewarding achievement.

Reproduced from *Team Development Games for Trainers* by Roderick R. Stuart, Gower, Aldershot

Please Join Our Team

Summary
- Suitable for any number of participants.
- Teams plan an advert which would attract the right person to join their present work team. This is offered to other teams, and a composite advert is produced. The composite is then displayed and used for comparisons and so forth during the course.

Objectives Assertiveness, communication, diagnostic, influencing, team development.

Materials
- Copies of the team briefing sheet.
- Flip charts, paper and pens.

Timing 45–60 minutes.

Procedure
1. Form teams, hand out the team briefing, and ensure that all participants understand the requirements.
2. Run the activity through the three stages.
3. Post the finished composite advert on a wall and refer to it during the course when necessary.

Commentary Ideal as an introductory activity for diagnostic or team development courses. It establishes what the ideal team member or team leader should be like, and you can therefore compare this picture at any stage with the current team position and determine what needs to happen to influence team members towards that ideal.

Variations None.

Team briefing: Please Join Our Team

Imagine that you require another person to join your team, initially as an ordinary team member to help cope with the workload, and also as a possible future team leader. Make this assumption concerning the underlying philosophy of your organization: that if people are treated considerately, developed through training, and given the opportunities to grow, they will fully repay the organization in terms of positive and effective effort.

Stage 1

Working in your own team, compile an advert for such a person. Include a broad description of the duties (keep this brief), then an outline of the package you would offer to attract the right person, and finally how you would expect the person to contribute to the team development itself. Your advert is to appear in an appropriate national newspaper. Produce your final advert on a flip chart.

Stage 2

Show your advert to the other teams, and explain your thinking behind the words used, and the terms and requirements stated.

Stage 3

Working within the main group, take parts of each team advert and draw up a composite advert that could be displayed on the wall of your present location as a reminder of the 'ideal team member' or 'ideal team leader'.

Reproduced from *Team Development Games for Trainers* by Roderick R. Stuart, Gower, Aldershot

Polybricks

Summary
- Suitable for any number of participants, with a minimum of 8.
- Teams watch a demonstration in which four individuals are invited to reproduce a design (using simple polystyrene cut-outs) which is created and explained to them by one of the four. The teams then plan, rehearse and complete their own version of the activity in front of other workshop participants.

Objectives Communication, diagnostic, feedback, listening, problem solving, team development.

Materials
- Copies of the observer's notes sheet.
- Four sets of simple polystyrene cut-out bricks of different shapes, each brick measuring about 10 cm × 5 cm × 2 cm. Each set should contain between 9 and 12 bricks, which can be whatever shapes the trainer decides, provided that the sets are identical.

Timing 45–60 minutes.

Procedure
1. Form teams of 4–5 members.
2. Introduce the game by discussing and recording on a flip chart some of the issues of using oral communication, such as the need for feedback, confirmation, assumptions, different interpretations of language, and use of jargon. Issues recorded on the flip chart can then be used to draw out additional learning points during the course.
3. Invite a member from each team (maximum four) to arrange and then sit at desks with their backs to each other, so that they can hear but not look at the other desks.
4. Hand out a set of the bricks to each person. Select one person to design and describe at the same time any shape or pattern using his or her bricks, whilst the remaining three volunteers replicate the same pattern on their own desks. No questions are permitted: all communication is one way – from the designer. The remainder of the group act as observers. They are asked not to comment, but simply to observe and then fill in the observer's sheet in as much detail as they can. (They often laugh, though, and this can be used in the review to illustrate the effect of non-verbal feedback.)

5. After about 7 minutes (or when completed), stop, thank the participants, briefly discuss what happened, and then tell each team that they are to go away, decide who in their team will be the communicator, and plan how they will carry out the activity as a team "to a perfect conclusion", given 5 minutes to perform.

6. Give the teams 10 minutes to plan, and then bring them back into the room. Each team then carries out the activity. Other teams watch, and then give brief feedback on the effectiveness of each team's performance.

7. On completion, teams return to their own area to review their own performance, using appropriate prompts (e.g. recorded notes, earlier verbal comment), check lists (see pp. 256–267) and feedback given by other teams.

8. As a follow-on-activity, teams should consider the effectiveness of oral communication at work, and plan how it can be enhanced.

Commentary The game demonstrates a simple model of communication – formulation, transmission, reception and interpretation – and is effective for a wide range of groups. It can be a very powerful experience, especially for the individual selected to be the communicator first time round. It appears very simple, yet most of us find it difficult to be concise and clear in our description of shapes. Learning points which flow from the game include: the need for feedback (verbal and non-verbal); the development of jargon as shorthand; the development of a common language within teams; and the learning which comes from observation and review of common experiences.

Variations When teams carry out the activity, any of the following variations can be introduced:

- The recipients of the communication are permitted to say Yes or No to show that they understand the instructions given by their communicator.
- At any stage, one recipient nominated by the team can ask any question. Others must remain silent.
- The Trainer records the communicator's voice, and then asks him or her to replicate the pattern whilst listening to his or her own instructions.
- Team members can ask whatever questions they wish whilst trying to follow the communicator's instructions.
- A team member describes his/her completed pattern before the other recipients have seen it. The original communicator listens to the total feedback, then describes any amendments necessary.
- Draw a pattern on paper, and then ask the communicator to replicate that pattern.

161

Observer's notes: Polybricks

As you watch the demonstration, think about the four main aspects of communication contained in the model, and write down your observations within each box, adding also at the bottom your comments on feedback instances and observations. Remember that the communicator and the recipients are affected by the audience's reaction to what is happening. Do not interfere or make comments during their performance.

Formulation
Transmission
Reception
Interpretation
Feedback instances and observations

Queen's Time

Summary
- Suitable for any number of participants.
- This activity is based on the idea that time can be halved simply because an individual states that it shall be so (e.g. the Red Queen in Lewis Carroll's *Through the Looking Glass*). People working for an organization would be required to plan and carry out their work in half the time previously available, and hence would need to prioritize their tasks and eliminate all timewasters. Teams are asked to consider their previous working week and then make changes to their future working week to satisfy the requirements of such a proclamation.

Objectives
Application, communication, diagnostic, influencing, team development, time management.

Materials
- Copies of the team briefing sheet.
- Flip charts, paper and pens.

Timing
45–60 minutes.

Procedure
1. Explain that the purpose of this activity is to oblige teams to consider critically how they spend time at work, in the context of a theoretical situation where time is halved. Hand out the briefing sheet.
2. Teams complete the activity.
3. Teams present their conclusions to the remainder of the course.
4. Lead a discussion on potential time-saving strategies at work and what actions could be taken to make more effective use of time. Brainstorming could be introduced as a very effective technique here.

Commentary
This activity naturally lends itself to any course on managing time, but it is also valuable as a diagnostic vehicle for teams to review how they spend time interacting at work. Individuals often have a distorted view of the relative amount of time used for different aspects of work and this can lead to heated discussions. Another value is that it will help to better organize future work and share tasks in ways which bring benefits to all involved.

Variations
None.

Team briefing: Queen's Time

In *Through the Looking Glass*, the Red Queen could have made the following proclamation (or, as she preferred to say, "memorandum"):

"Henceforth, everyone in my Queendom will spend half their time in normal activities, and half their time in mirror-image activities that will reflect everything in the original activity, but beginning at the end."

Team activity
Assume that you have received the above proclamation. You understand it to mean that, from now onwards, you will have only half the time you previously had to complete your work. You will need to prioritize your tasks, and eliminate all non-essential activities.

Consider, therefore, how you spent the last working week, and how you will spend the next working week. Make a list on a flip chart of all activities that you now consider non-essential.

Put your revised work-time plan on a flip chart, and be prepared to defend both this plan and your list of non-essential activities to the course group.

Sell Us a Sport

Summary
- Suitable for any number of participants.
- Teams work, first, to select four sports which they consider could be introduced into their own organization, and then to develop and present their option to the other participants.

Objectives
Assertiveness, communication, decision making, influencing, presentation, team development.

Materials
- Copies of the team briefing sheet.
- Copies of sports illustrations.
- Flip charts, paper and pens.

Timing
45–60 minutes.

Procedure
1. Form teams.
2. Hand out the briefing sheets and illustrations and ensure that individuals and teams understand the game.
3. Allow 15 minutes for teams to decide on their selection.
4. Reassemble in one group, decide on the sequence of presentations, and complete these.
5. Separate teams to review their own performance and individual contributions.

Commentary
Although I have indicated that this game uses 45–60 minutes, I have also found it valuable in a shortened version, in which teams are given 7 minutes to make their choice, followed by 3 minutes to prepare and give their presentation.

Variations
None.

Team briefing: Sell Us a Sport

On the attached sheet there are illustrations of a number of sports.

Working as a team, select four sports that you consider could be introduced into your own organization as a "preferred sport" and for which the organization would be prepared to pay for most of the setting up, training and development, and so forth. Individuals would be able to take part in the preferred sports at a discount, and departmental teams would compete annually for a cup which brings with it weekend breaks at a hotel, all costs paid, for competitors and partners.

Now decide how you would "sell" these sports to the committee which will decide on the sports to include. (The committee in your case are the other teams on the course.) Develop a 2-minute presentation that will sell your selection.

You have 15 minutes to complete this task.

Reproduced from *Team Development Games for Trainers* by Roderick R. Stuart, Gower, Aldershot

Illustrations of sports: Sell Us a Sport

1. American line dancing

2. Croquet

3. Ten-pin bowling

4. Cricket

5. Angling

6. Lawn tennis

7. Archery

8. Golf

9. Football

Reproduced from *Team Development Games for Trainers* by Roderick R. Stuart, Gower, Aldershot

Sell Your Team

Summary
- Suitable for any number of participants.
- Teams produce a presentation that will sell their team to another organization which is involved in the same type of work as our present teams.

Objectives   Communication, diagnostic, influencing, presentations, team development.

Materials
- Flip charts, paper and pens.

Timing   30–45 minutes.

Procedure
1. Form teams.
2. Ask teams to complete Stages 1, 2 and 3 of the activity.
3. Teams draw lots to decide the running order, and then ask teams to make their sales presentations.
4. Ask teams to complete Stage 4 of the activity.
5. Lead a discussion on the conclusions which teams have reached in Stage 4 of the activity.

Commentary   This is an excellent activity for assessing the relative motivational levels of teams through the strength of the sales presentation they make on their own behalf. In this way, the current level of team development can be assessed, and ways of making the team more effective at work considered. You need to take care that teams do not become unrealistic in singing their own praises and abilities. You might, for example, ask for recent evidence to substantiate their claims.

Variations   None.

Team briefing: Sell Your Team

In this activity you are asked to sell your work team to another organization. Other teams on the course will make a decision whether you are a "Good buy" or "Goodbye". The interested organization is looking for a team to work in the same locality as you are at present, on similar terms and conditions of service. The team will carry out a similar work function to your present one.

Stage 1
Working as a team, produce a summary of the most effective aspects of your team that would appeal to another employer who operates in the same commercial market as you do at present.

Stage 2
Select one member who can make an effective selling presentation for the team. You have 5 minutes to present your team and a case for it in the new organization. You will be questioned on your presentation and may be asked to justify any aspect of it.

Stage 3
After hearing all the sales presentations, the teams decide which *one* of the other teams they would buy. If there are only two teams, your course trainer will decide.

Stage 4
Working in your original team, discuss your team performance and consider the following questions:

● How clear was the task for individual members?
● How did your team decide on (a) the selling points, and (b) your presenter?
● How did you draw out and evaluate the contributions of individual members?
● How strongly were you all agreed and committed to the final solution?
● What would you do differently as a team next time with a similar task?

Summarize these points on a flip chart as a record and for future reflection.

Reproduced from *Team Development Games for Trainers* by Roderick R. Stuart, Gower, Aldershot

So What are You Going to Do About It?

Summary
- Suitable for any number of participants.
- Towards the end of a course on team development, individuals and teams plan future actions which will transfer the learning into the workplace and improve effectiveness.

Objectives   Application, feedback, presentations, team development.

Materials
- Copies of the team briefing sheet.
- Flip charts, paper and pens.

Timing   60–90 minutes.

Procedure
1. Form teams to include individuals who will work together in the future.
2. Complete the activity.
3. Lead a session to review the activity and summarize the main learning points.

Commentary   This activity is valuable in three ways: as a consolidation of learning during the course; as an evaluation of the effectiveness of the course; and as an action planning session. The last item – action planning – can then be reviewed in future courses to measure progress.

Variations   None.

Team briefing: So What Are You Going to Do About It?

We have now reached the end of this particular development programme. However, for you as an individual and the team in general, what you do after this course is crucial to the ways in which you become more effective.

Stage 1
Working within your teams, compose three or four phrases which capture the main changes you plan for the future as a result of this programme. Include individual and team changes where possible.

Stage 2
For each of the planned changes, decide the following:

- What you will do, individually and collectively (your action plans).
- What further support you need to help you (e.g. in terms of additional learning, resources, time and so forth).
- When and how you will be able to point to success in your action plans.

Put your ideas on a flip chart, and select one person to present these to the main group.

Stage 3
Present your action plans to the main group. Each team should use no more than 5 minutes for this presentation.

Reproduced from *Team Development Games for Trainers* by Roderick R. Stuart, Gower, Aldershot

Star Performer

Summary
- Suitable for any number of participants.
- Teams decide on the criteria they would use to select the person on the course who has contributed most. Individuals then vote for the person whom they think has made the most significant contribution.

Objectives   Assertiveness, feedback, influencing, team development.

Materials
- Copies of the team briefing.
- Copies of a blank voting paper – one per participant – on which the agreed criteria can be listed.
- Copies of a blank form – one per participant – on which the individual scores can be recorded.
- Flip chart, paper and pens.

Timing   30–45 minutes.

Procedure
1. Elect one leader for the whole group.
2. Agree the criteria to be used in making the choice of the winner. Write these criteria on a flip chart.
3. Each individual completes a voting slip, marking his or her vote against each of the criteria. (The leader has *only* a casting vote, if it is required.)
4. The leader takes these away, adds up the votes, and reaches a result on the overall winner (using his or her casting vote if necessary). At the same time, each individual predicts how many votes he or she will receive on the selected criteria. This is recorded by each individual, and need not be communicated to the others!
5. The leader returns, and gives each individual a slip of paper showing the number of votes he or she has received for each criterion. The leader announces the winner of the competition, and awards the prize.
6. If necessary, the leader explains briefly why he or she chose the winner if a casting vote was necessary. Individuals are given the opportunity to volunteer how close the team's score is to their own predicted personal score. This can be followed in a subsequent session by more detailed and relevant feedback for individuals, delivered in small groups.

Commentary This can be an enjoyable activity to precede the final review of a course, and also a powerful way of drawing teams together. A prominently displayed bottle of wine, chocolates or other acceptable small prize adds to the feeling that we are rewarding a member of the group for their contributions and support.

It can be used to rehearse assertiveness for a previously non-assertive team member, by giving him or her the leadership role. It can also enable individuals to recognize how their contributions are valued by the group, leading towards a feedback session.

Be aware however, that not all groups will reach the stage of openness which is needed to make this successful. I have had groups who have been reluctant to vote for any one person for the prize, but instead have voted to share it. In such a case, accept their decision, but insist that they construct a set of criteria by which a team leader can openly praise the efforts of his or her team members.

Variations None.

Team briefing: Star Performer

For this activity, you have to elect one leader. He or she will manage the process of selecting one member of the group who is seen to have made the greatest contribution to the course. The winner receives a Star Performer Certificate and a prize to take away from the course (purchased from contributions from all participants).

Criteria for selection
The leader should list criteria selected by the group, plus one selected by him- or herself. Some examples of possible criteria include the following:

- Meaningful involvement.
- Original contributions.
- Support given to other members.
- Intellectual input.
- Willingness to accept positive feedback.

At least *four* criteria must be adopted, and there is no weighting to be allocated to individual criteria.

Ground rules

- Each person has one vote on each of the criteria chosen by the course members. These votes can be used for different people in the group. For example, you could vote for one person on, say, Original Contributions, but for a different person on Support.
- The leader must be included as a candidate for the prize.
- The individual who wins the most votes on the combined criteria is to be named by the leader.
- No individual may vote for him- or herself.

Straight from the Horse's Mouth

Summary
- Suitable for any number of participants.
- Team members, acting individually, consider a picture of Pegasus, the mythical flying horse, and decide which of the descriptions of various parts of the horse apply to each of the other team members. Team results are then collated to produce a wider response, which is offered to the individuals concerned. The team then consider how they can develop parts of the horse which appear to be missing from the current behaviour of the team as a whole.

Objectives   Application, communication, diagnostic, feedback, listening, team development.

Materials
- Copies of the team briefing sheet.
- Flip chart, paper and pens.

Timing   45–60 minutes.

Procedure
1. Introduce the activity as an opportunity for individuals to offer and receive feedback from team members on their contributions to team efforts, using a different approach to known models of team roles.
2. Form teams of those who have worked together.
3. Complete all four stages of the activity as shown on the briefing sheet.
4. Lead a discussion in which all teams are invited to share their action plan for the future development of their teams.

Commentary   This is a valuable activity for offering and receiving feedback when teams know each other very well and have moved into the stage of development where they are committed to open, honest observations on each other. Ensure that the feedback is couched in positive terms so that weaknesses are seen as areas of underdevelopment, rather than as personality traits incapable of improvement!

In stage 4 of the procedure, you may find it useful to capture the team action plans to increase effective working and co-operation under two headings: what individuals will do, and what the team collectively will do.

Variations   None.

Team briefing: Straight from the Horse's Mouth

In this activity you are asked to think about some of the roles which individuals play within the team, and offer them feedback on what you have observed. Rather than use any of the various models such as the Belbin Team-Roles, you are asked to imagine that your team is represented by Pegasus, the Greek mythical flying horse (see illustration).

Stage 1
Working entirely by yourself, consider each of the other team members in turn, and record which parts of Pegasus you think the person represents in the way they act within the team. You may use each part of the horse as many times as you wish – or not at all. Include yourself in the list.

Stage 2
Working as a team, now collate all entries for each individual and put these onto a flip chart.

Stage 3
Once the list is completed, each member of the team should examine the entries made for them, and reflect on what this feedback has to offer them in terms of the way they operate and interact in the team. They may ask for clarification, but should not attempt to change the observed recording.

Stage 4
As a team again, consider the ways in which you currently work together, and plan ways in which the team can be developed to make it more effective. Look, in particular, for parts of the horse which seem to be missing or could be developed to make the team more effective.

Reproduced from *Team Development Games for Trainers* by Roderick R. Stuart, Gower, Aldershot

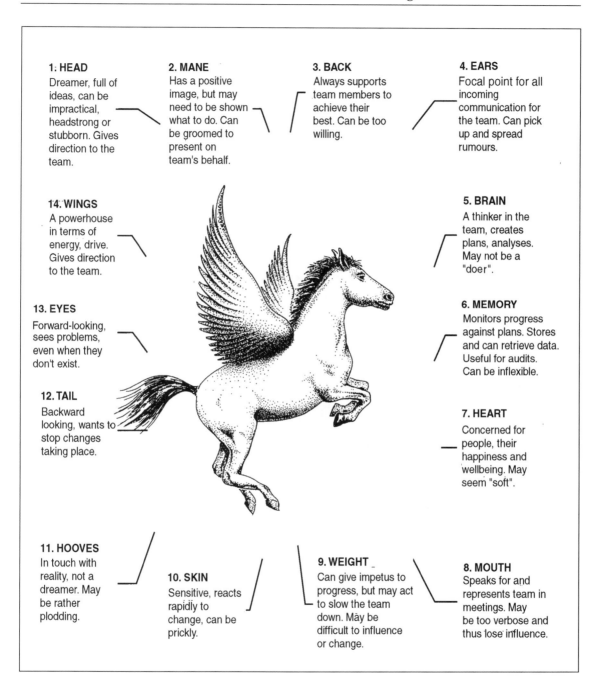

1: HEAD
Dreamer, full of ideas, can be impractical, headstrong or stubborn. Gives direction to the team.

2. MANE
Has a positive image, but may need to be shown what to do. Can be groomed to present on team's behalf.

3. BACK
Always supports team members to achieve their best. Can be too willing.

4. EARS
Focal point for all incoming communication for the team. Can pick up and spread rumours.

14. WINGS
A powerhouse in terms of energy, drive. Gives direction to the team.

5. BRAIN
A thinker in the team, creates plans, analyses. May not be a "doer".

13. EYES
Forward-looking, sees problems, even when they don't exist.

6. MEMORY
Monitors progress against plans. Stores and can retrieve data. Useful for audits. Can be inflexible.

12. TAIL
Backward looking, wants to stop changes taking place.

7. HEART
Concerned for people, their happiness and wellbeing. May seem "soft".

11. HOOVES
In touch with reality, not a dreamer. May be rather plodding.

10. SKIN
Sensitive, reacts rapidly to change, can be prickly.

9. WEIGHT
Can give impetus to progress, but may act to slow the team down. May be difficult to influence or change.

8. MOUTH
Speaks for and represents team in meetings. May be too verbose and thus lose influence.

Reproduced from *Team Development Games for Trainers* by Roderick R. Stuart, Gower, Aldershot

SuperAnt

Summary
- Suitable for any number of participants.
- Teams consider a typical team member, list all of the work-related demands placed on that individual, and change his or her physical attributes so that they are better able to cope with the incoming demands.

Objectives   Application, communication, diagnostic, team development.

Materials
- Copies of the team briefing sheet.
- Flip charts, paper and pens.

Timing   30–45 minutes.

Procedure
1. Form teams to include those who have worked together for some time.
2. Give teams the briefing sheet, and ask them to complete the activity.
3. Teams present their particular list of pressures on individuals, the picture of the fully prepared team member, and their action plan for the future.

Commentary This light-hearted activity enables everyone involved to become aware of each individual's perceived incoming pressures, and their views on changes which could be made to meet these demands and ease their situation. You may find that some of the pressures mentioned are coming from other members, thus providing an opportunity for team development in your review. There are also likely to be issues concerning communication, formal and informal, outside as well as inside the team.

Variations   None.

Team briefing: SuperAnt

Background

At work, we all experience many demands on our time, energy, thinking power, resourcefulness, initiative, relationships with other team members, and so on, as well as demands on our skills and abilities. These demands are communicated to us through our senses – sight, hearing, taste, smell, and touch – and they influence the way we feel, think and act.

Activity

Consider a typical – not actual – member in your work team, and list on a flip chart all the demands that might be placed on that person from whatever direction they may appear (including pressures from other members in the team). Ensure that the views of all team members are recorded.

Now change this typical individual's physical attributes (e.g. add another pair of hands if you think this is needed!) and add appropriate defensive clothing, so that the individual will be better able to cope with the incoming demands. Record these changes on the flip chart in order to build up a picture of the fully prepared and competent team member – a superant!

Finally, prepare a short presentation on your superant to be delivered to the course group.

Reproduced from *Team Development Games for Trainers* by Roderick R. Stuart, Gower, Aldershot

Symbols of Your Work Team

Summary

- Suitable for any number of participants.
- Teams select illustrations of animals which they consider appropriate to the qualities of their working team, and present their option to the course. All the teams then consider how closely the selected illustrations mirror the goals of their organizations.
- This activity is most suitable for groups from the same organization or similar work-related operations, but can easily be adapted for general use.

Objectives   Assertiveness, diagnostic, influencing, listening, team development.

Materials

- Copies of the team briefing sheet.
- Copies of sheet of illustrations.
- Flip charts, paper and pens.

Timing   30–45 minutes.

Procedure

1. Explain the purpose of the activity, and hand out the team briefing sheet and sheet of illustrations.
2. Form teams and complete the activity.
3. Lead a discussion which considers the various illustrations chosen and the match between these and the goals, culture and values of participants' organizations. Highlight differences and identify actions which can be taken to improve the match.

Commentary   This activity is an ideal way of introducing teams to the concept of organizational goals and culture. The selected illustrations may be seen as a light-hearted symbol, but the subsequent search for reasons and examples leads quickly in to an authentic consideration of a required match.

Variations   Instead of illustrations of animals, you could ask teams to describe the appropriate clothing for teams, the appropriate historical setting for teams, or an appropriate geographical region.

Illustrations of animals: Symbols of Your Work Team

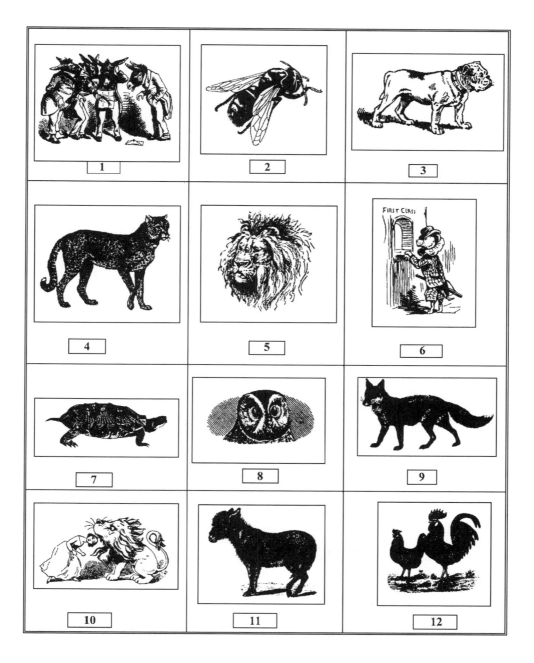

Reproduced from *Team Development Games for Trainers* by Roderick R. Stuart, Gower, Aldershot

Team briefing: Symbols of Your Work Team

Stage 1
Working as a team, select four of the attached pictures of animals which you consider best cover the essential qualities of your work team.

Stage 2
Prepare a 2-minute defence of the pictures or animals you select that will explain to the group both why you have made the choices you have and why you have disregarded the others.

Stage 3
Nominate one member of your team to present your case.

You have 10 minutes in which to make your selection and prepare the case for presentation on a flip chart.

Team Climate Survey

Summary
- Suitable for any number of participants.
- Individuals complete a detailed questionnaire loosely linked to the task, team and individual overlapping circles model of leadership. This activity is designed to diagnose the current state of the team in terms of how members feel. The analogy is climate, in which members feel either warm or cold. Subsequent stages of the activity draw in the views of all members of the team, and present these views to others on the course.

Objectives Communication, diagnostic, team development.

Materials
- Copies of questionnaire.
- Copies of list of statements.
- Copies of team briefing.
- Flip charts, paper and pens.

Timing 45–60 minutes.

Procedure

1. Explain that the purpose of this activity is to assess the mental climate within which the team work. Individuals will complete a questionnaire anonymously so that they can be completely honest in their responses. Replies will be collected, collated and reviewed. The team will decide what actions can be taken to improve the atmosphere within the team.
2. Hand out two copies of the individual questionnaires, and have them completed. Individuals retain one copy for their own record. The other is handed in for further action in the team activity.
3. Collate all views of the team on a flip chart and complete the first stage of the team activity.
4. Teams present their findings to the remainder of the course.
5. You summarize the course findings, and draw out common actions which can be taken at work to improve the atmosphere.

Commentary This activity can be a very valuable way of enabling individuals to express their feelings on the current state of the team in a non-threatening environment. It can also be used to assess the mental climate of teams working together to carry out their usual occupational roles, or where teams have been formed during a course and have begun to develop a team identity. The use of two copies of the questionnaire is optional, since in some circumstances the views of individuals are well known to all. However, some individuals feel happier when their views are confidential, and naturally, this confidentiality must be respected by the trainer. An important stage of this game is the review stage, when future actions are planned to improve the team climate.

Variations   In hot climates the trainer could reverse the cool–warm poles. The descriptors of the climate could be changed to indicate, for example, an atmosphere of barrenness–fertility or stunted–rapid growth.

Questionnaire: Team Climate Survey

Note: This is essentially an individual activity.

Section 1
If someone asked you to show how "warm" or "cold" the climate is within your team where would you put your mark on this chart?

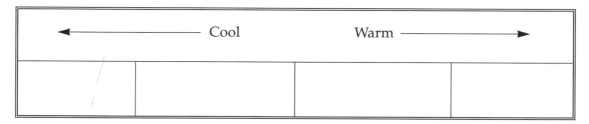

Section 2
Now complete the attached survey to add more information to your first impression above. Just tick (√) the box which reflects your own view to show whether or not you agree with the statements.

Section 3
Having completed as many items as you can on the questionnaire, add up the columns to show how you rate the team. Count one point for each tick (√) in each column and insert the totals for each column into the first part of the diagram. Then transfer your scores to the second part – the boxes immediately below – to show your detailed analysis.

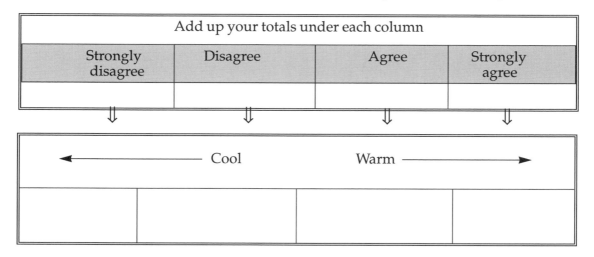

Reproduced from *Team Development Games for Trainers* by Roderick R. Stuart, Gower, Aldershot

Team briefing: Team Climate Survey

Stage 1
Each individual completes *two* copies of the questionnaire handed out by the retainer, returning one completed copy and retaining the other for his or her own record.

Stage 2
The team now considers the individual views of all team members, and decide where the coolest aspect of the climate survey has occurred. Look for explanations for this coolness, and make realistic recommendations which would lead to a warming of the atmosphere.

Stage 3
Put your team recommendations on a flip chart, and select one member to present these recommendations to the other participants on the course. Make sure your presenter has rehearsed the main points that the team want to make.

List of statements: Team Climate Survey

The achievement of the work of the team

Strongly disagree	Disagree	Statement	Agree	Strongly agree
....	....	(a) Work-related decisions are shared as far as possible.	....	....
....	....	(b) Team members stand in for each other and share peak workloads.	....	....
....	....	(c) Everyone in the team knows what is happening and what is planned.	....	....
....	....	(d) Individuals perform their preferred team roles (e.g. as in Belbin's Team Roles) and are seen to make a positive contribution to work.	....	....
....	....	(e) The leadership style used within the team is respected, with individuals willing to offer feedback in an honest and open way.	....	....
....	....	(f) Work patterns are agreed within the team and are flexible.	....	....
....	....	(g) Work achievement is reviewed positively and constructively.	....	....
....	....	(h) Team members monitor the quality of work performance.	....	....

Reproduced from *Team Development Games for Trainers* by Roderick R. Stuart, Gower, Aldershot

Strongly disagree	Disagree	Statement	Agree	Strongly agree
....	....	(i) Work-related changes for the team are accepted and put into action.	....	....
....	....	(j) Team members clearly see themselves as part of an effective team.	....	....
....	....	(k) Team members set and maintain their own standards of behaviour and code of conduct.	....	....
....	....	(l) Team members openly praise the achievements of others, and offer honest and constructive feedback for improvements and developments.	....	....
....	....	(m) Conflict is resolved positively and constructively without harming future relationships.	....	....
....	....	(n) All members are committed to maintain and improve the status of the team.	....	....
....	....	(o) There is an atmosphere of openness, trust and mutual support.	....	....

Reproduced from *Team Development Games for Trainers* by Roderick R. Stuart, Gower, Aldershot

Individual motivation and commitment

Strongly disagree	Disagree	Statement	Agree	Strongly agree
....	....	(p) Individuals are motivated to do what is needed without having to be told.	....	....
....	....	(q) Individuals demonstrate a commitment to achieving team goals.	....	....
....	....	(r) Individuals share confidences and feel able to discuss personal matters as well as work-related issues.	....	....
....	....	(s) Individuals are encouraged and supported by other team members in developing new skills to enhance their career prospects.	....	....
....	....	(t) Individuals are keen to learn and develop skills which support the team effort.	....	....

Reproduced from *Team Development Games for Trainers* by Roderick R. Stuart, Gower, Aldershot

Team Development Goals

Summary
- Suitable for any number of participants.
- Individuals are asked to consider twelve goals of team development and rank order the goals. Teams then collate the work of individuals and draw up a team rank order of the same goals. They then brainstorm ways in which they can achieve the most important goals.

Objectives   Application, brainstorming, communication, diagnostic, influencing, managing team boundaries, team development.

Materials
- Copies of individual and team briefing sheet.
- Copies of list of goals.
- Flip charts, paper and pens.

Timing   45–60 minutes.

Procedure
1. Use this activity early in a team development programme so that the outcomes can be referred to during the programme and can be used as a yardstick for evaluating the continued development of the teams over time.
2. Explain the purpose of this activity, and the importance of individuals completing the rank order of goals before the teams meet.
3. Hand out the list of goals, and give individuals time to complete this.
4. Form the teams, select team leaders, and ask the teams to complete their part of the activity. A short break before the brainstorming session helps to separate the analytical dimension from the creative dimension.
5. Lead a review session with emphasis on the outcomes of the brainstorming phase. Teams will have achieved different results in their brainstorming, and the review can provide additional actions for all teams.

Commentary   All of the goals are valid in terms of developing teams, and it is likely that teams will want to merge two or more goals in one rank order. There can be value in this, but there is also the disadvantage that the more general the goal becomes, the less defined and achieveable are the actions to be taken.

The activity has two dimensions: the step-by-step convergent dimension leading towards an agreed list; and the creative divergent dimension of the brainstorming session. The short break suggested above helps individuals to adjust from one dimension to the other.

Variations None.

Individual and team briefing: Team Development Goals

This activity is designed to help you to establish and clarify the goals for your own team development. In the attached list there are twelve goals, and the objective is to decide the most important five of these goals for your own team.

Stage 1
Working individually, select what you personally consider are the five most important goals for the future development of your current work team. Place these in rank order, with the most important first.

Stage 2
When all team members have completed Stage 1, the team leader should collect the lists, add up the individual score for each goal, and mark the total team scores on the flip chart. (*Note:* The lowest total shows the most important goal.) Discuss the results and make any agreed changes that the team believes will make it more effective in the future.

Stage 3
After a short break, brainstorm ways in which you can collectively achieve the goals you have set within a reasonable and feasible time frame in the future.

List of goals: Team Development Goals

		Your own rank order	*Team rank order*
1	A shared understanding of the need to work as a team and the benefits which derive from this understanding for each individual.	....	....
2	A better understanding of each team member's role in the work team.	....	....
3.	A better understanding of the team's purpose and role within our organization.	....	....
4.	More effective communication among team members.	....	....
5.	Greater co-operation and sharing of resources within the team.	....	....
6.	A clearer understanding of how the team can work together in the future.	....	....
7.	More effective ways of working through problems affecting work and interpersonal relations.	....	....
8.	The ability to be more productive and effective in the workplace.	....	....
9.	More effective team training and development activities.	....	....
10.	More effective feedback to individuals on personal contributions and development to meet the team standards and objectives.	....	....
11.	More effective ways of developing the team and reviewing how we are "growing" together.	....	....
12.	A more effective strategy for managing boundaries with other teams.	....	....

Reproduced from *Team Development Games for Trainers* by Roderick R. Stuart, Gower, Aldershot

Team Draughts

Summary
- Suitable for up to 12 participants. Additional participants can be invited to be observers.
- Teams play a game of draughts using a board which is projected onto an overhead projector screen.

Objectives   Assertiveness, communication, diagnostic, influencing, team development.

Materials
- Copies of the team briefing.
- An overhead projector.
- A transparent draughts board produced to fit the overhead projector.
- Two sets of different shaped draughts (twelve per set), or three normal sets of draughts and boards if you decide to play the variation.

Timing   30–45 minutes.

Procedure
1. Prior to the game, construct a draughts board using normal transparency materials. Number and letter the board up and down as shown, to make identification easier. Set out the draughts as for the normal game of draughts.
2. Form teams of 4–6 players on each team. The teams need to be far enough apart to discuss strategy in private, and able to see the developing game on the overhead projector screen.
3. Offer the teams the rules and ensure that they understand the game.
4. Play the game, giving each team no more than five seconds to state each move. Failure to do so means loss of the move, and the opposing team make their next move.
5. Play the game three times to produce a winning team.
6. Teams review their team and individual performances.

Commentary   A simple game which can be used to introduce communication within teams, influencing skills by individuals, the different levels of risk taking by individual members, and the effects of win–lose results on teams.

Variations Use three normal draught boards, one set up within each team circle, and the third as a master set some distance between the competing teams. Team members must approach the master board, make a move, note the consequences, then return to their own team and update their own set. A different player makes the next move.

Board illustration: Team Draughts

	1	2	3	4	5	6	7	8
A	○		○		○		○	
B		○		○		○		○
C	○		○		○		○	
D								
E								
F		□		□		□		□
G	□		□		□		□	
H		□		□		□		□

Reproduced from *Team Development Games for Trainers* by Roderick R. Stuart, Gower, Aldershot

Team briefing: Team Draughts

In this game of team draughts, your team must collectively decide which move to make next. You have *five seconds* only in which to decide and make your next move. Failure to meet that deadline means loss of that move, and the initiative passes back to your opponents. Only one person in your team can call out a move.

Note: This game differs from draughts in the following ways:

- The first team to *give away* all their counters and kings is the winner.
- Failure to capture an opposing counter or king when a capture is possible means the game is conceded to the opposing team.

Reproduced from *Team Development Games for Trainers* by Roderick R. Stuart, Gower, Aldershot

Team Effectiveness Review

Summary
- Suitable for any number of participants.
- Teams consider their own work team and measure effectiveness in three overlapping areas: achieving the work, developing the team, and motivating and developing individuals. Having assessed their current state, teams are asked to plan and explain how they can become more effective.
- This activity is most suitable for groups from the same organization or similar work-related operations, but can easily be adapted for general use.

Objectives
Communication, conflict management, decision making, diagnostic, influencing, team development.

Materials
- Copies of the team briefing sheet.
- Copies of survey sheet.
- Flip charts, paper and pens.

Timing
45–60 minutes.

Procedure
1. Explain the purpose of the activity, which is to examine the current state of development of the work team, and make decisions on how to improve working practices within the team.
2. Individuals complete the review by themselves. You must ensure that they concentrate on issues within the team which are work related, rather than on the ways in which team members interact socially.
3. Form teams of individuals who are part of the same work team and complete the activity shown in the attached review sheets.
4. Lead a discussion with the intention of summarizing and consolidating the learning points and making decisions on future actions required of the teams.

Commentary
This is a practical and work-focused activity which enables teams to look at issues at a time and place which enable the central issues to be discussed. The review is likely to go beyond the relatively analytical and

198

unemotional level of considering work achievement, and to encompass interpersonal relationships in the workplace. You need to be sensitive to this, and guide individuals towards actions and solutions that help to resolve conflict and do not damage the future development of the team in any way.

Variations   None.

Team briefing: Team Effectiveness Review

The individual

The attached survey, which you should complete by yourself, has been designed to help you to review the current way your work team operates, and to consider how to improve its effectiveness in the future. As you complete it, try as far as possible to concentrate your thoughts and analysis on the issues within the team that are related to work, rather than on the ways in which people relate to one another (e.g. ignore personality clashes unless these affect the team's work).

The team

1. Working as a team, consolidate the views of everyone in the team from the individual review they have just completed. Transfer these to a flip chart, ensuring that all contributions are recorded.
2. Now analyse the flip chart, looking for common issues, and prioritize the issues in terms of "importance to the effective working of our team".
3. Decide what actions you can take as a team and what recommendations you can make that will achieve the following objectives:
   (a) To resolve any difficulties or conflict which have arisen between team members over work-related issues. Where these cannot be resolved quickly, decide how the individuals involved should work towards co-operation and agreement on these problems.
   (b) To enable the team to operate more effectively in a *win–win* way.
   (c) To provide opportunities for further review and open discussion of unresolved issues. Plan dates when these discussions can take place, and decide who will take responsibility for actions in the interim period.

Survey: Team Effectiveness Review

Complete the following survey by noting in the final column each aspect of the area involved is being achieved by your team, providing examples where possible.

Main area involved	Description	Comment
Achieving the work	● Work is clarified and clearly defined.	
	● Work is planned.	
	● Appropriate resources obtained.	
	● Work and resources allocated.	
	● The pace and quality of work is controlled.	
	● Work is measured and reviewed, and performance checked against targets and plans.	
	● Plans are modified to meet new situations.	

Reproduced from *Team Development Games for Trainers* by Roderick R. Stuart, Gower, Aldershot

Developing the team

- Your team 'case' or views are represented accurately to outside departments and divisions.

- Standards of work are accurately set.

- Team discipline and direction are maintained.

- Team identity and spirit is built up.

- The team is encouraged, motivated and praised as a group.

- Team members are selected to contribute and complete specific team projects.

- Effective communication is maintained and developed within the team.

- Team skills and effectiveness at work are developed, monitored and reviewed.

Motivating and developing individuals

- Personal problems are sensitively and fairly discussed and resolved.

- Individuals are encouraged and supported.

- Individual work performance is regularly reviewed.

- Achievement is recognized.

- The individual's abilities and skills are recognized and used effectively at work.

- Individuals are encouraged and supported to develop themselves in areas not directly related to their work.

Reproduced from *Team Development Games for Trainers* by Roderick R. Stuart, Gower, Aldershot

Team Leadership Styles

Summary
- Suitable for any number of participants.
- Individuals complete an inventory which describes a continuum of leadership styles from hierarchical to participative. They then collate individual responses, consider the current style in the work team, and decide how effective this will be for future work practices.

Objectives Communication, diagnostic, feedback, leadership, team development.

Materials
- Copies of individual and team briefing sheet.
- Copies of the continuum of contrasting leadership styles sheet.
- Flip charts, paper and pens.

Timing 45–60 minutes.

Procedure
1. Form teams of those who have worked together.
2. Hand out the continuum of leadership styles sheet and ensure that individuals understand the terms used.
3. Invite individuals to complete Stage 1.
4. Ask teams to complete Stage 2.
5. Ask teams to present their findings to the course. Other teams comment on the proposed actions.
6. Summarize the findings, drawing attention to any issues brought out by teams.
7. Teams withdraw to their own room, and draw up a set of action points they can implement at work, taking into account the comments and observations of others.

Commentary This activity can be valuable when the organization is undergoing change or team working is being introduced. The traditional hierarchical model of leadership may no longer be appropriate, and because the team leader works within the team he or she must adopt a different style. If individuals and/or teams have difficulty in completing a particular item you can highlight this as an area for development in their team.

When participants on the course are from different organizations, you can use the inventory to establish current styles in the organizations and suggest changes the participants would welcome or see as beneficial.

The inventory can also be used with other games in the book.

Variations None.

Individual and team briefing: Team Leadership Styles

Stage 1: individual preference
The attached sheet lists a number of actions and ways of behaving for team leaders. Each pair of actions indicates contrasting styles of leadership.

Place a tick (√) against one or other of the statements in each pair, indicating at which end of the continuum *you* would prefer your team leader to be. (e.g. in pair (a), if you consider that a team leader should be hierarchical, and have a strong sense of superior–subordinate, then tick (√) the *left-hand* column).

When you have completed your personal preference you will have the opportunity to discuss it with others in your team.

Stage 2: team preference
Working as a team, put all the team responses on to a flip chart, by counting the number of responses for each end of the continuum.

When you have completed this, analyse the responses and decide if there is a clear style of leadership operating in your team. Then consider:

1. Whether the present style is going to be effective for the future.
2. How you would go about modifying the style in order to become more effective as a team.

Select one person to present your findings to the work group.

The continuum of contrasting styles: Team Leadership Styles

A leader **of** a team	A leader **within** a team
(a) Hierarchical in outlook, has a strong concept of superior–subordinate.	(a) Fits into the team and has a defined set of work objectives in addition to that of team leader. .....
(b) Task oriented, thinks in terms of *what* must be achieved. Controls flow of ideas.	(b) Innovative, imaginative, no rigid adherence to the plan. Accepts ideas from team. .....
(c) Plans *what* needs to be done.	(c) Co-ordinator of activities. .....
(d) Practitioner of one-way communication towards each individual.	(d) Communicates *within* the team (e.g. uses team briefings, consults, explains). .....
(e) Remains as the communication focal point (like the spokes of a wheel).	(e) Becomes part of a communication network within the team. .....
(f) Sets the work objectives for the team.	(f) Consults and agrees work objectives. .....
(g) Regulates, enforces organizational policies/procedures.	(g) Works within the group to uphold organizational procedures, rules and policies. .....
(h) Monitors and evaluates work output.	(h) Encourages individuals to monitor and improve own quality of work. .....
(i) Sets down rules of behaviour, enforces disciplines.	(i) Gains acceptance for group rules. .....
(j) Provides "the" solution to problems.	(j) Accepts that others in the group may have better solutions to problems. .....

Reproduced from *Team Development Games for Trainers* by Roderick R. Stuart, Gower, Aldershot

*A leader **of** a team*	*A leader **within** a team*
(k) Acts as the prime source of resources and knowledge, represents the group.	(k) Encourages the use of other sources of support and assistance. .....
(l) Retains the leadership role in group discussions, filters ideas and suggestions.	(l) Accepts and performs his/her most effective team role. .....
(m) Structures the working environment for the group.	(m) Encourages the group to structure the working environment. .....
(n) Less comfortable discussing feelings, sensitive issues, needs of others.	(n) Supports the creation of an open atmosphere in which feelings can be expressed. .....
(o) Decides the application of work techniques, methods of working.	(o) Develops and uses skills of team members. Flexible in work methodology. .....
(p) Determines team relationships, the "mood" of the team.	(p) Supports team members in building the team identity. .....
(q) Assesses work effectiveness.	(q) Demonstrates respect for individuals in the team. Enables individuals to reflect and assess their own achievements. .....
(r) Accepts responsibility for success or failure.	(r) Shares responsibility with team. .....

Reproduced from *Team Development Games for Trainers* by Roderick R. Stuart, Gower, Aldershot

Tell Us a Story

Summary
- Suitable for any number of participants, with a minimum of 9.
- This very active game involves teams in translating and then acting out a children's story written in Welsh. Teams decide on their game strategy, and then purchase information on translated pages or lines of the book, or make up the story and rely on other criteria to gain highest points.

Objectives Assertiveness, communication, creativity, influencing, team development, time management.

Materials
- Copies of a children's story book: Marian Jones, *Sanau Newydd Sali* (*Sally's New Socks*), ISBN 0948469 196; available from HMSO, The Friary, Cardiff CF1 4AA (Tel: 01222 395548). Ideally, one copy for each participant is required, but the set can be reused many times.
- Copies of team briefing.
- Copies of each page of the story – one complete set for each team – with a line-by-line translation alongside the original Welsh.
- Flip charts, paper and pens.

Timing 90–120 minutes.

Procedure
1. Hand out the story books, together with the information on scoring. Explain the game.
2. Ask teams to write down how they would award the marks to other teams for accuracy and presentation of such a story. (i.e. what criteria they would use). The scoring sheets are not made public at this stage.
3. Send teams to separate rooms to complete the translation and prepare their playlet.
4. Decide the order of presentation, and then ask each team to act out their playlet. Other teams score each presentation, but do not reveal their scoring until all presentations have been completed.
5. Teams reveal how they have scored each presentation. You then deduct points for any information purchased by each team. You can now declare the winning team.
6. Teams review their performance in separate rooms.

Commentary This game has proved popular with a very wide range of groups and can become hilarious since teams relish the opportunity to outact all others! The story line is simple, but provides ample scope for the players to project themselves and dress for the part. It is particularly valuable as a climax to a longer course where teams have learned to work together. Teams need time to unwind and review their performance, which again helps to develop a team identity. The scoring is not intended to be taken too seriously.

Variations Any foreign language short story could be used, together with a translation. Marian Jones has written a number of excellent variations, and all are available through HMSO, The Friary, Cardiff. (Remember to get the translation as well.)

Team briefing: Tell Us a Story

Outline
In this game, you are asked to translate a story from Welsh into English. Having translated the story, you then prepare and deliver an enactment of the story. Other teams will score your performance, using the team information shown below. The team with the highest number of points wins the game.

Stage 1
To enable you to score the acting of other teams, use 10 minutes to draw up a scoring sheet indicating what criteria you would use to award marks for presentation, accuracy and entertainment value. You will use your scoring sheet later, but for the present, do not show this to the other teams.

Stage 2
You have 30 minutes to complete the translation, purchasing whatever information you decide would be helpful. Remember that information purchased will cost you points, as follows:

Item of information	Cost in points
The translation for each complete page	15
The translation for any line in the book	4

Stage 3
You now have 30 minutes to select your narrator, the characters in the playlet, and rehearse.

Stage 4
Take part in the playlet, scoring the acting of other teams, and team performance reviewed as directed by your trainer. The scores you may award are as follows:

Aspect of presentation	Marks awarded
Accuracy of storyteller	Up to 50 points
Entertainment value	Up to 50 points
Active involvement (per member of team)	25 points

Reproduced from *Team Development Games for Trainers* by Roderick R. Stuart, Gower, Aldershot

Story and translation: Tell Us a Story

Page 1

"Beth sydd yn y parsel?"
gofynnodd Huw Bob Lliw.
"Wyth o sanau i Sali Sws,"
atebodd Twm Crwn.

"What is in the parcel?"
asked Huw Every Colour
"Eight socks for Sally Sws,"
answered Twm Crwn.

Page 2

Neidiodd Twm Crwn
i ganol y mor mawr.
Sblash!

Twm Crwn jumped
into the big sea.
Splash!

Page 3

Nofio, nofio, nofio.
i waelod y mor mawr.
Tybed ble mae Sali Sws.
yn byw ... meddyiodd Twm Crwn.

Swim, swim, swim,
To the bottom of the big sea.
I wonder where Sally Sws
lives ... thought Twm Crwn.

Page 4

"Mae Sali'n byw draw
yn y fan acw,"
meddai Neli'r Pysgodyn Jeli,
"ond gwylia di ...
mae creaduriaid cas
iawn o gwmpas."

"Sally lives
over there,"
says Nelly the Jellyfish,
"but watch out ...
there are some nasty
animals about."

Page 5

Roedd Neli'n iawn.
Roedd y Sardin Blin,
Marc y Siarc
a Ffranc y Cranc
yn gwylio Twm Crwn.

Nelly was right.
The angry sardine,
Mark the shark,
and Frank the Crab
Were staring at Twm Crwn.

Page 6

"Tyrd a'r sanau i mi!"
gwaeddodd Ffranc y Cranc yn flin.
Roedd Twm Crwn druann
yn crio a chrio a chrio ...

"Give me the socks!"
shouted Frank the Crab angrily.
Poor Twm Crwn was
crying and crying ...

Permission to reproduce *Sanau Newydd Sali* in this text has been given by the Curriculum and Assessment Authority for Wales (ACAC) as holders of the copyright.

Reproduced from *Team Development Games for Trainers* by Roderick R. Stuart, Gower, Aldershot

Page 7

Clywodd Pry Cry Twm Crwn
yn crio.
"Pry Cry ydw i.
Wedi dod i'ch helpu chi,"
meddai.

Pry Cry heard Twm Crwn crying.

"Pry Cry am I.
I've come to help you,' said he.

Page 8

"Ali Bali Shali Ba!" gwaeddodd Pry Cry.
"I mewn i'r hosan, Sardin Blin
I mewn i'r hosan Ffranc y Cranc!
I mewn i'r hosan, Marc y Siarc!"

"Ali Bali Shali Ba!" shouted Pry Cry.
"Into the sock sardine!
Into the sock, Frank the Crab!
Into the sock, Mark the Shark!"

Page 9

"Tyrd gyda mi, Twm Crwn,"
meddai Pry Cry.
"Awn i chwilio am Sali Sws."

"Come with me, Twm Crwn,"
said Pry Cry.
"We'll go and look for Sally Sws."

Page 10

"Dyma hi!'
"Helo Sali Sws yr octopws,
Dyma wyth o sanau i ti."
"Diolch yn fawr, Twm Crwn.
Diolch yn fawr."

"Here she is!"
"Hello Sally Sws the octopus,
Here are eight socks for you."
"Thank you very much, Twm Cryn.
Thank you very much."

Page 11

"Mae'r sanau'n hyfryd!
Mae'r sanau'n Lliwgar!
Mae'r sanau'n gynnes, gynnes!
meddai Sali'n hapus.

"The socks are lovely!
The socks are colourful!
"The socks are warm and warm, warm!"
said Sally happily.

Page 12

"O, Twn Crwn bach,
tyrd a sws i mi,"
meddai Sali.
"O na, mae'n bryd i mi fynd,"
meddai Pry Cry.
"Hwyl fawr!"

"Oh, little Twm Crwn,
give me a kiss,"
said Sally.
"Oh no, it's time I went,"
said Pry Cry.
"Goodbye!"

Reproduced from *Team Development Games for Trainers* by Roderick R. Stuart, Gower, Aldershot

They're Dancing to Our Tune

Summary
- Suitable for up to 20 participants.
- Teams decide on a piece of music which they think describes the essential qualities of their work organization. They then plan, rehearse and deliver a short musical production to persuade other teams to adopt their tune as the organization's anthem.

Objectives Communication, diagnostic, influencing, presentation, team development.

Materials
- Copies of the notification sheet (to be distributed prior to the course).
- Copies of the team briefing sheet.
- Paper and pens.
- A tape recorder for each team.
- Each team will require the use of a separate room for rehearsal.

Timing 45–60 minutes.

Procedure
1. Form teams (if possible by putting together participants who already know each other or whom you expect to see operating as a team in the future). No leaders are needed.
2. Teams decide on their own selection, then plan and rehearse their musical production.
3. Hold the musical productions.
4. Each participant votes for the production which he or she finds the most entertaining and persuasive to be the organization's anthem.
5. Teams review their own performance in terms of individual contributions, collective actions, time management, and communication skills.

Commentary This can be a valuable activity to help developing teams to come together during a course. Timing is fairly important – ideally, when the individuals have settled down and are looking for a demonstrative session. Naturally, the fun factor is high, but it should not be allowed to take over; reminding participants of the need for a quality production, rather than plain slapstick may be helpful in this respect. The value of the activity as a diagnostic study can be judged from the degree of commitment demonstrated by individuals in raising their own choices, taking part and so on.

Variations   None.

Prior notification to individuals: They're Dancing to Our Tune

Note: This notice should be sent or given to all intended course participants at the same time as the course enrolment instructions.

During the forthcoming training event, you will be asked to join a team and decide on one tune or piece of music that you would select as the anthem for your current organization.

Before you arrive for the training course, please take the trouble to record on a tape cassette two or three pieces of music that you consider might be appropriate for this purpose and bring the tape cassette with you. The trainer will provide suitable equipment on which to play your choices of music.

Team briefing: They're Dancing to Our Tune

Between you, you will have a number of different pieces of music, all of which have been selected to reflect the organization in which you work. Working as a team, consider each in turn, and then decide collectively on one final choice. The main criterion for your choice should be that the piece of music can serve as an image or anthem that reflects the best qualities of a modern business organization.

Now plan a short dramatic presentation (no longer than 5 minutes) that you will deliver to the course members, and which you hope will persuade them that yours is the anthem for the future.

Each member of your team must take some active part in the dramatic musical production.

Reproduced from *Team Development Games for Trainers* by Roderick R. Stuart, Gower, Aldershot

Tykes Versus Romans

Summary
- Suitable for up to 15 participants.
- Two teams are involved in a negotiation activity in which the local population (the Tykes) are seeking to negotiate with the resident Roman army on future community relationships, now that peace has been secured in the northern region of Britain.

Objectives
Communication, conflict management, feedback, influencing, listening, team development, team leadership.

Materials
- Copies of the information sheet.
- Copies of the team briefing sheet.
- Copies of the map of the town.
- Flip charts, paper and pen.
- Each team will require a separate room in which to work.

Timing
60–90 minutes.

Procedure
1. Form teams, if possible teaming up those participants who normally work together. Select observers as appropriate. Each team needs to elect one negotiator (who will also act as team leader), one assistant negotiator, and one scribe who will minute and record all discussion and decisions reached at the negotiating sessions.
2. Give each team a short time to read the general background information.
3. Teams now establish their own negotiation objectives.
4. Bring the Tykes and the Romans together in an exploratory meeting, during which each team finds out the other's general position.
5. Teams return to their own room, and redefine the objectives they think they can now realistically gain during subsequent negotiations.
6. Ensure that both teams know the time constraint (15–20 minutes) for the actual negotiations.
7. Run the negotiation activity.
8. Observers offer feedback to the elected team leaders. This can be done as a joint session, whilst team members take a short break.

9. Teams retire to their team rooms to reflect on their performance.

Commentary This is one of those activities which can be particularly successful. As the negotiations develop, there are countless opportunities for you as a trainer to observe examples of the activity objectives in operation. Observers can be a valuable reference point for the review stages. The activity also offers an opportunity to dress the part, since teams are allowed to design and wear distinctive clothing (one of acknowledged team characteristics). Valuable emphasis is placed on the team leadership development objective, especially as the elected leader will be faced with a number of typical leadership challenges (e.g. information overload, delegation, influencing, time management, securing agreement to a policy, and so forth).

Variations None.

Information given to all teams: Tykes Versus Romans

The following information is common knowledge in the town, and is given to all concerned. Like all information, some will be valuable, whilst the remaining may need to be treated with caution.

Negotiation purpose
The citizens (Tykes) want to renegotiate with the military (Roman soldiers) the decennial (ten-year) agreement whereby the military are allowed to remain in the town. Without this agreement the military would be asked to leave the town. Many changes have taken place in the last ten years, which has seen the dawn of peace after the Hadrianic uprising was put down.

Town
The town is called Municipium Aqua Vey, a sort of dilapidated modern town. There are approximately five hundred Tykes living in the town, excluding children. The town is situated in north Yorkshire, about five miles north of Ripon.

Military

1. There are about five hundred soldiers in the town, made up of mounted infantry, a few engineers and signalling station specialists. Altogether they make up a cohort, and this cohort is part of the Augusta Legion, stationed (in terms of modern-day Yorkshire) near Ripon. (Incidentally, the Roman ramparts can still be seen, about three miles north of Ripon on the A6108, half-way between North Lees and North Stainley, on the left-hand side of a long sweep of road which follows the line of the dried up River Vey.)
2. The soldiers' morale is low, because the local soothsayers are forecasting a bleak future for them, with no regular money being paid for their services.
3. Many soldiers are married, even though legally they are banned from marrying until they reach the rank of centurion. If the military leave the town, their wives must be left behind, destitute.
4. The citizens depend on the soldiers to quarry stone locally and bring it in to the town.
5. If the military do leave the town, no one will be left to defend it against marauding raids from the direction of the east coast, from the tribes to the west (Lancashire!) and from the Brigantes in the north.
6. The military worship a god called Coventina, and celebrate by dressing the wells around the town with flowers and other offerings, which usually end up down the well. This causes friction and ill feeling between townfolk and soldiers in the town since the water is now hardly drinkable.
7. There is also a military secret society dedicated to the god Mithras. The local prefect has a room dedicated to Mithras in the temple, from which all women and non-members are strictly barred. The society causes the citizens serious problems, since it holds power over financial matters in the town.

Community relations

1. The soldiers stable their horses in the town, in the square behind the Forum (the town hall). There is a huge pile of horse manure near the Forum.
2. The soldiers make an infernal din when they practise drill formation on the parade ground, particularly when they beat their swords against their shields.
3. The soldiers' supply of meat is driven into the town every Wednesday, which is the same day as the citizens are busy transporting their goods out of the town to the nearby market town (via the East Gate).
4. Hang gliders have injured many citizens, when the soldiers practise take off and landing routines on the parade ground.
5. The canal section of the River Vey is stagnant and smelly. In the past, it was part of the defences of the town, but now it needs filling in and ramparts building in its place. Only the military have the skills to do this.
6. The amphitheatre is badly vandalized since some soldiers of the XXI Legion ran riot at the last games. The civilian dignitaries want this repaired in time for the annual Das Shera celebrations for the local god of the dales.
7. The pottery kilns smell of sulphur, and give off black smoke when the soldiers are burning bits of skin left over from the tanning of their leather equipment. Old bones are also burned by the auxiliaries (local militia attached to each cohort of regular soldiers).

Economic factors

1. The region is mainly farming, and is self-sufficient in terms of iron goods. Merchant traders sail up the Ouse to York, and travel on with pack horses to Municipium Aqua Vey in order to barter glass, wines, and leather goods for locally mined iron ore and wool.
2. The citizens are enjoying an increasing standard of living, with only the annual 'Cult of the Standard' tax to pay in to the coffers of the military. This tax pays for the defence of the local area. The tax per household is ten denarii (sufficient to keep an average household in fuel costs for a year).
3. The soldiers each spend about twenty denarii per year in the town on entertainment, goods and services.
4. It will cost about one thousand denarii to rebuild the amphitheatre, and three thousand denarii to make good the fortifications after draining the canal section of the Vey.

Reproduced from *Team Development Games for Trainers* by Roderick R. Stuart, Gower, Aldershot

Team briefing: Tykes Versus Romans

You will have been asked by your trainer to assume the roles of either the townsfolk (commonly called Tykes) or the military (the Roman soldiers).

Your team task is to negotiate with the other team, and achieve as many of your objectives as you can during the negotiating part of the activity. Each team must establish their own negotiation objectives after reading the information sheet. Remember that the purpose of any negotiation is to arrive at a point where everyone feels they have a bargain. Failure will leave your team facing a very insecure future (e.g. the town will be left vulnerable to attacks from warring tribes in the area, and from the seafaring Vikings of Northern Europe).

In order to carry out the negotiating session, each team must have a senior negotiator (team leader), an assistant negotiator, and one scribe who will minute and record all discussion and decisions agreed during the negotiating sessions. A team member will also need to record your team objectives on a flip chart. These objectives will be reviewed at the end of the activity.

Reproduced from *Team Development Games for Trainers* by Roderick R. Stuart, Gower, Aldershot

Map of Municipium Aqua Vey in AD 159

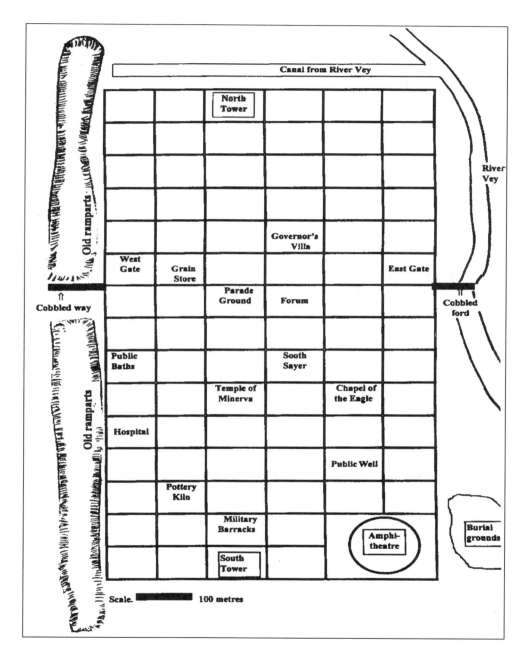

Reproduced from *Team Development Games for Trainers* by Roderick R. Stuart, Gower, Aldershot

Viking Chess[1]

Summary
- Suitable for up to 12 participants.
- Teams plan their strategy around their copy of a board game (which is a cross between draughts and chess), then compete against another team on a master set. Members take turns and report back to their team on the results of their move.

Objectives   Communication, decision making, influencing, team development, team leadership.

Materials
- Three boards made, or hand-drawn on a flip-chart sheet, to the specification shown in the illustration.
- Three sets of coins, each consisting of three denominations of coins: one coin for the King; eight of a different denomination for the defenders; and twelve of a third denomination for the attackers. As an alternative, counters of three different colours can be used.
- Copies of team briefing sheet.
- Copies of objectives and rules sheet.

Timing   30–45 minutes.

Procedure
1. Form two teams of 5–6 players each. Select leaders if necessary. Other participants act as observers.
2. Set out the master board using only eight defenders and twelve attackers as shown on the illustration. The King occupies the central square.
3. Give teams 5 minutes to read the instructions. They then set out their own board.
4. Play the game.
5. If you have used observers, ask them to offer their feedback to the teams. Teams review their performance, with emphasis on the contributions made by members, the processes of decision making, and the effectiveness of their team communication.

---

[1]Permission to use this version of the *Viking Game* in this text has been given by Past Times, a trading division of the Historical Collections Group Plc.

Commentary A very simple yet effective competitive game, which is great fun to play. It is a version of the Viking Game (obtainable in the UK through Past Times: telephone 01993 770440) that has been simplified in order to complete the game in a shorter period of time. Very good as a communication game where individuals need to follow instructions and note a visual picture to be transferred back to their copy of the board. You may wish to consider asking teams if they want additional time as they approach the notified time limit (15 minutes). Teams will react differently, depending on their current game position. Teams who think they are winning will not require more time, and vice versa. When the allotted 15 minutes have elapsed many teams find themselves in a different end position to that which they had anticipated during the activity, and ruefully conclude that additional time would have been an advantage, or that the extra time requested and granted in fact lost them the game.

Variations None.

Board: Viking Chess

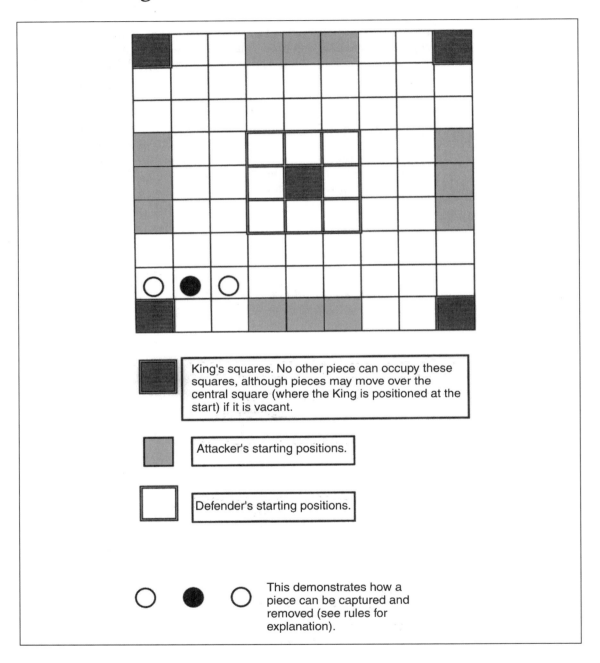

King's squares. No other piece can occupy these squares, although pieces may move over the central square (where the King is positioned at the start) if it is vacant.

Attacker's starting positions.

Defender's starting positions.

This demonstrates how a piece can be captured and removed (see rules for explanation).

Reproduced from *Team Development Games for Trainers* by Roderick R. Stuart, Gower, Aldershot

Objectives and rules: Viking Chess

- The objective for the *attackers* is to capture the King. For the *defenders*, it is for the King to escape and occupy one of the corner squares.
- The attackers make the opening move.
- Pieces including the King can move in any direction *up or down* the board and *across* it, for as many squares as is decided upon and possible.
- No piece may move diagonally, or jump over another piece on the board.
- A piece is captured and removed from the board when the opposing team manages to place one piece on either side of it. For example, in the illustration on the board, the black piece would be taken off when the second white piece moved to box it in.
- The King can take part in manoeuvres to capture an attackers' piece.
- The King is captured when he is boxed in on all sides. The central square (King's square) can be used as one of the four boxing-in sides if required.

Reproduced from *Team Development Games for Trainers* by Roderick R. Stuart, Gower, Aldershot

Team briefing: Viking Chess

1. Set up the game on your copy of the board. Use coins as symbols of the players. The trainer will set up a master board with an identical layout of pieces.
2. You will require three denominations of coins (value is unimportant): one coin for the King; eight of a different denomination for the defenders; and twelve of a third denomination for the attackers.
3. The rules are simple (see attached sheet), but if your team consider that there is need for a ruling on any aspect of the game, you must call for time out to discuss and agree the rule changes with the other team. (For example, are teams to co-operate and observe each other's moves on the master board; or should they only be allowed to approach the board *after* their opponents have made their move, thus having to work out the move that has been made, which increases the complexity of the task?)
4. Decide on your team strategy for either defending or attacking the King. For each move, one of your team must approach the master board and make a move. Having made the move, that person comes back to your table, reports on the outcome, and your team decide on the next move. Another team member makes this next play, and each team member takes turns to make a move during the game, so decide on your team order.
5. Follow the game as it unfolds by replicating the moves on your copy of the playing board.
6. The game is played for 15 minutes maximum unless either the King is captured earlier or he escapes into the sanctuary of one of the corner squares. If there is no result within 15 minutes, the winning team is the one which has captured and removed more of the opposing forces.

Reproduced from *Team Development Games for Trainers* by Roderick R. Stuart, Gower, Aldershot

Want a Job?

Summary
- Suitable for any number of participants.
- Individuals produce a profile of themselves which could be used as part of a CV if they were applying for a job within their own team. This is then offered to other team members, who make a simple selection decision.

Objectives
Assertiveness, communication, feedback, influencing, team development.

Materials
- Copies of individual briefing sheet.
- Paper and pens.
- A separate location is required for each team, where they can talk in private.

Timing
45–60 minutes.

Procedure
1. Invite individuals to produce their own profile using the guidelines in the briefing sheet.
2. Form small teams of three participants each, who then move to their own location and make a selection decision for each person in their team.
3. The team members remain in their own location, and offer feedback to each member of their team.
4. Lead a discussion with all participants on the course, concentrating on general development issues which have come out of the feedback session. List these issues and establish how they can be addressed in the work environment.

Commentary
Valuable towards the end of a course when participants are more receptive to constructive criticism from team members, and more aware of development or training needs. The outcomes of your course discussion can also provide useful information about how individuals perceive their own future development needs.

Variations
None.

Individual briefing: Want a Job?

Stage 1

Working entirely by yourself, produce a profile of yourself that could be used as part of your CV if you were applying for the job of either team member or team leader in your present occupational work group or course team. Produce the profile under the following three headings:

- What you can offer in terms of the work involved.
- How you would expect the job to satisfy your personal motivational needs.
- What you could contribute to the further development of the team.

Stage 2

Listen to each individual in your team as they present their profile and market themselves for the job. Ask whatever questions you need for clarification, and then make your own selection decision in one of the following categories:

- *Category 1*   The job is yours. When can you start?
- *Category 2*   The job could be yours. We will let you know when we have completed the interviews.
- *Category 3*   At present, we feel that you need further development in certain of the stated requirements before we could consider you for the position.

Stage 3

When all members of your team have presented their profile and the selection decisions have been announced, offer feedback to each of the job applicants to clarify and explain your decision.

What Do You Advise?

Summary

- Suitable for any number of participants.
- Teams are asked to become management consultants and improve the motivation of teams in their own organization. They are then asked to produce a simple prompt card which can be issued to all managers as an *aide-mémoire* when motivating people. Finally, they are asked to draw up an action plan under three headings: the resources needed, the actions to be taken, and the criteria to measure success.

Objectives   Application, communication, creativity, diagnostic, presentations, team development, team leadership.

Materials

- Copies of team briefing sheet.
- Flip charts, paper and pens.

Timing   60–90 minutes.

Procedure

1. Form teams.
2. Explain the purposes of the activity, including the importance of keeping their efforts focused on work and the motivation of people within the organization. Ensure that teams understand the model they will use for Stage 4 in the briefing sheet.
3. Distribute the briefing sheet and complete the activity.
4. Lead a discussion on the outcomes from Stage 4.

Commentary   This is an activity which is designed to be applied to work situations and to promote more positive motivation. Hence it has value in developing team leaders as well as teams. The simple process model (i.e. the action plan in Stage 4) is particularly valuable to help teams organize their thinking for this and other planning activities. The outcomes need to be applied to work situations and reviewed at a later date to monitor the actions being taken.

Where participants are not in the same work team, or belong to different organizations, the value of the activity is that each participant is able to take away a simple 3-part model which they can apply within their own work environment. In this case, however, the action plan in Stage 4 will obviously change, and will instead incorporate general motivational factors under the following main headings: intrinsic motivation from the *work itself*; extrinsic motivation through *recognition of success*; fairness and clarity of *administration* at work; *personal development* of the individual; *relationships at work*; and *job security* (see separate list).

Variations   None.

Team briefing: What Do You Advise?

Assume that your team are management consultants called in by your organization to suggest ways in which work teams can become more positively motivated, and also to recommend what criteria you would use to measure motivation within work groups.

Stage 1
Working as a team, list all possible causes of poor motivation in work groups. Ensure that you include your own work team.

Stage 2
Now produce a simple 'prompt card' that could be given to team members and team leaders, and which could be used as an *aide-mémoire* when motivating people.

Stage 3
Select one member of your team to present the results of both stages to the main group.

Stage 4
After you have given your presentation and heard those of other teams, return to your syndicate room and write an action plan for the next six to nine months which is designed to promote positive motivation within your own work team. Your action plan needs to cover three linked parts: the resources needed to implement the plan; the process or actions which will lead to the achievement of the objective; and the criteria to measure success (i.e. how you will be able to point to the effectiveness of the plan). Write down the criteria to measure success first, since this will influence what you do, and the resources you will invest in the plan.

Reproduced from *Team Development Games for Trainers* by Roderick R. Stuart, Gower, Aldershot

List of motivational factors: What Do You Advise?

Listed below are various motivational factors common to most work situations:

1. A sense of achievement from seeing the results or end products of my work.
2. Good work recognized within the company.
3. The ability to get totally involved in work.
4. Using my initiative to plan and carry out work.
5. Career advancement opportunities.
6. Opportunities to develop as an individual.
7. Company administration and working procedures which are seen to be fair.
8. Reasonable supervision of work.
9. Constructive and open relationships with my immediate line manager.
10. Reasonable physical working conditions.
11. A reasonable salary, relative to experience and abilities.
12. Constructive and open relationship with work colleagues.
13. The ability to have a personal life without work interruptions.
14. Constructive and open relationship with subordinates.
15. Job status.
16. Job security.

Reproduced from *Team Development Games for Trainers* by Roderick R. Stuart, Gower, Aldershot

Where are You Now?

Summary
- Suitable for any number of participants.
- Teams spend ten minutes mentally retracing their steps from the training location to another recognized location, then produce a set of instructions and a map setting out the route.

Objectives   Assertiveness, communication, influencing.

Materials
- Copies of the team briefing sheet.
- Flip charts, paper and pens.

Timing   20–30 minutes.

Procedure
1. Form teams.
2. Hand out the instructions.
3. Complete the activity.
4. Review the team processes, concentrating on the roles team members assumed informally.

Commentary   A light-hearted and non-threatening introductory activity, yet, surprisingly, this generates a great deal of noise and active involvement. The activity works well in locations where course participants have arrived at the training room from a car park, and move into the training location via reception areas, corridors and stairs.

Observers can be valuable since they can note influencing and assertive behaviour – in many cases such behaviour leads teams towards an inaccurate solution!

Variations   Any two locations separated by some distance can be substituted (e.g. two departments, geographical sites).

Team briefing: Where are You Now?

● Working as a team, mentally retrace your steps from here to the location given to you by your trainer.
● Write out instructions to that location, and draw a simple map to accompany your instructions.
● Include any instructions which would help people carrying a heavy object such as a box of materials.
● Reproduce the map on a flip chart, and select one member of the team to explain your solution to the whole course group.

Reproduced from *Team Development Games for Trainers* by Roderick R. Stuart, Gower, Aldershot

Who Are Our Competitors?

Summary
- Suitable for any number of participants.
- This game is designed to enable teams to compete or collaborate by taking degrees of risk in their dealings with each other. The teams represent two divisions of their company which export products to the same market, either by air or land.

Objectives Application, assertiveness, communication, conflict management, decision making, influencing, team development.

Materials
- One copy of the master scoring sheet.
- Copies of the team briefing sheet.
- Flip chart, paper and pens.
- Cardboard or wooden chips representing gold blocks. (Jenga game blocks are ideal. They can be purchased from retail games shops.)

Timing 45–60 minutes.

Procedure
1. Prepare the master scoring sheet beforehand.
2. Introduce the game as a vehicle to see which team can make the most profit for their own division. (At the end of each consignment, you will hand out blocks of profit, or take back losses, and enter the decisions on the master sheet, and display this sheet for the teams to see.) Hand out the briefing sheet, and let participants read this.
3. Form teams. Separate the teams so that they cannot overhear each other. Select and brief any observers you wish to use.
4. Give the teams 5 minutes to appoint representatives for meetings with the other team, and to read and understand the briefing sheet.
5. Play the game.
6. Review the strategies of each team, the effects of competition, conflict management within the teams, the role of the representative, the relevance and implications of the outcomes for work situations, and the actions they can take to enhance effectiveness at work.
7. Separate the teams, and ask each to review individual contributions.

Commentary In addition to developing team identity, this game can be valuable to focus awareness on "Who is our competitor?" at work. Often divisions or departments compete rather than collaborate, thus reducing production efficiency. They fail to recognize the interdependent nature of projects and changing work patterns. Hence the need to review and plan actions to enhance collaboration at work. The game highlights the level of competitiveness of individual participants and any conflict within the team, points which may need to be addressed in the review stage.

Variations   Have two separate companies rather than divisions of the same organization. Both companies can be affiliated to the local Chamber of Commerce, thus establishing a collaborative–competitive dimension.

Team briefing sheet: Who Are Our Competitors?

1. Read and make certain that you understand the following scenario and scoring system.

    Two divisions of your company send their products to the same overseas market. Their products can travel by land or by air. However, if one division delivers its product to the destination before the other, the late arrival makes a loss. Travel by land is slow, but guarantees delivery on the same train as the other product. This produces two blocks of profit. Air travel is faster, but if both products go by air, then both consignments will be lost in an air crash. This produces a loss of two blocks of profit for each team. If, however, one team send their product by air and the other team by land, the air travel team gains four blocks of profit, and the land travel team loses four blocks. The scoring system (in blocks of profit) is illustrated in the following diagram:

		Team A (scores in brackets)	
		Land travel	Air travel
	Land travel	(+2) +2	(+4) −4
Team B (scores without brackets)	Air travel	(−4) +4	(−2) −2

2. Your team represents one of the two divisions of the company. You have a total of ten consignments to deliver, and for each you can choose to travel by land or air.

    Reproduced from *Team Development Games for Trainers* by Roderick R. Stuart, Gower, Aldershot

    239

3. Working as a team, decide how you will send the first consignment. After 3 minutes, pass a slip of paper to the trainer stating your selected mode of transport. The other team will do the same. The trainer will then log both selections on a master sheet, and by examining this you will know whether or not your team have made a gain or loss. Return to your team to discuss and decide on the mode of transport for the next consignment as directed by the trainer. Repeat the process for all ten consignments.

Consignment	Decision time (minutes)	Travel choice Team A	Team B	Profits–losses Team A	Team B
1	3				
2	3				
3	3				
4 ☺	3 (meeting) 3 (decision)				
5	3				
6	3				
7	3				
8	3				
9 ☺	3 (meeting) 3 (decision)				
10 ☺	3 (meeting) 5 (decision)				
Final year profit or loss					

Note: ☺ the profit or loss is *doubled* for this consignment; ☺ the profit or loss is *multiplied by four* for this consignment.

Reproduced from *Team Development Games for Trainers* by Roderick R. Stuart, Gower, Aldershot

Index of games by objectives

Check lists for use in facilitating team development

In the notes below I have offered some suggestions for using the check lists contained in the book, which are intended for use by observers, and by other participants on the direction of the trainer. However, these notes are simply a reflection of the ways in which I myself have used the lists, and I am certain that you as a trainer will decide how best to use them to fulfil your own objectives, modifying them to suit your particular requirements for specific courses. I consider them as a series of tools that can be used to help participants reflect on a learning experience, to add dimensions to the various skills being learned, and to provide consistency when you are developing personal skills over a period of time.

Team leadership development check list

This can be used by nominated observers during a game to focus on the behaviour of a team leader, and also by team leaders and team members to reflect on the learning experience after the event. Experience using the check list suggests that not all the items will be covered in a single event, but as it is used over time, all items appear. Perhaps the only guidance I would offer is to be sensitive to the situation in which the check list is being used – there should be a supportive and learning environment where the appointed leader is playing a role which may be new and unfamiliar.

Individual development check list

This approach to offering feedback enables the participants to use their own language in which to couch the feedback. Hence it is appropriate for whatever levels of educational attainment or sophistication are current within the group, and there is no requirement for you as the trainer to offer interpretations of the concepts used. It is an active approach in which the person receiving the feedback is personally involved in writing up the observations from the team, and placing these observations in either a negative or positive domain. Participants will find it valuable to clarify what was meant and what was heard, since the meaning behind the message can easily be lost or distorted by inappropriate language, either verbal or non-verbal. Additionally, we often hear what we want to hear, rather than what the transmitter of the message intended.

Feedback on communication skills check list

This check list is offered for use when presentation skills training takes place during a team-building event. There are two aspects which I would suggest that you should bear in mind. First, when using the check list, ensure that the participants recognize the general level of skill within the group and rate individuals accordingly. Second, dissuade participants from following a natural tendency to go for the mid-point on the rating scale.

Feedback on team presentation check list

This check list is designed to be used when teams, rather than individuals, make a presentation. I have found that the activity of planning, preparing and delivering the presentation is itself a valid way of developing the team. The list is therefore valuable for reflecting on team performance once the team has made its presentation. It is also useful as a vehicle to help teams plan their presentations. The twelve aspects follow the broad chronological timing throughout the presentation, but are not rank-ordered in terms of importance.

Assertiveness check list

This check list can be used whenever assertiveness development features as one of the objectives of your course. It should be completed by team members and offered to the individual concerned at an appropriate time and in a supportive environment, such as the team syndicate room.

Reflective check list

This check list is designed to enable a team to reflect on its performance during any of the games in the book and focus on the broad questions, "Were we working as a team?" and "Do we share the view that we are a team?" Individuals may have perceptions which are not shared by others in the team, and this can be established by recording the individual responses on a master chart showing all dimensions.

To preserve anonymity and increase honesty in the responses, I have suggested that the completed copies of the check list should be collected and reissued at random. I also usually offer participants two copies of the list to complete, one of which they retain in order to compare their own responses with the overall team response.

Team development check list

This check list is completed by teams after they have taken part in a game. Part of the value accrues from the participants' own choice of adjectives to describe their performance.

Team leadership development check list

Instructions for use by an observer

Review the check list before the activity begins, to familiarize yourself with the various statements. Tick each behaviour which you observe the leader carry out at some time during the activity. Make any notes that you consider may help you when you offer feedback to the leader. During your feedback session with the leader, always refer to the actions of "the leader", and not the individual by name – we are not assessing individuals, but observing particular examples of leadership behaviour!

Instructions for use by a team player

The check list may also be used in the same fashion by team players to reflect on the performance of their appointed leader.

Behaviour	Yes	No
Task facilitation		
1. Explained the task objectives to all team members.	.....	.....
2. Sought advice and ideas from team members.	.....	.....
3. Made a plan and told all members what this was.	.....	.....
4. Allocated tasks to individuals and delegated authority.	.....	.....
5. Checked completed tasks against the plan.	.....	.....
6. Controlled the tempo of work and checked the constraints.	.....	.....
7. Avoided getting over involved with particular tasks.	.....	.....
Team development		
8. Had an enthusiastic manner.	.....	.....
9. Maintained discipline or control as appropriate.	.....	.....
10. Ensured that all team members knew what was going on.	.....	.....
11. Worked towards creating a distinct team identity.	.....	.....

Behaviour	Yes	No
Individual development		
12. Listened to and encouraged ideas from individuals.	.....	.....
13. Explained why ideas could not be used	.....	.....
14. Used particular skills of individuals.	.....	.....
15. Praised individuals for their efforts.	.....	.....

Individual development check list

Receiving feedback

Purpose

The purpose of this activity is to enable you as an individual to listen to feedback offered to you by colleagues and other members of a course on team development. Having heard and written down the feedback, you are naturally free to reject it or to accept and use it in the future. You will also be able to employ this technique with your own team members.

Learning points

The following learning points can be observed in the activity:

● Differing perceptions of the same words or ideas.
● The need for care when giving and receiving information.
● Dangers of misinterpretation (e.g. use of words, body language, indistinct speech, tone of voice, and so forth).

Process

In order for you to evaluate the feedback correctly, you should adopt the following procedure:

● Stand in front of those offering the feedback.
● Write down the feedback on a flip chart that has been prepared to show two columns: *positive* and *negative*.
● Decide into which of the two columns to put each item of feedback. You may also decide to put it across both columns.
● Simply write down exactly what the individual says who is offering the feedback, without changing any part of it and *without* interruption from you (i.e. either to explain or to defend yourself).
● Once you have listed all items of feedback, then it is your turn to explain to colleagues why you put each item of feedback in to a particular column, together with any further clarification of your words and actions that you may wish to offer.
● Keep the flip chart until after the course and consider it again when you are back at work. You will then be able to make a more rational and objective judgement on the value of the feedback, and what actions you need to take.

Feedback on communication skills check list

The following rating scale can be completed to show the relative level of skill in each dimension, where 1 reflects a very low level of skill and 5 shows a very high level.

Oral skills

Dimension of skill	1	2	3	4	5
(a) Fluency of expression, using words in their easiest and most appropriate way.					
(b) Matching language level, complexity and use of jargon to the audience.					
(c) Handling questions, comments, observations from the audience.					
(d) Clarity of sound, projection of voice.					
(e) Presenting a convincing argument.					
(f) Flow of speech, pace, level of enthusiasm.					
(g) Non-verbal communication: confidence, facial expression, calmness, posture, movement of hands, gaze.					

Use of flip chart or other presentational materials

Dimension	1	2	3	4	5
Legibility					
Conciseness					
Use of colour					
Level of language					
Presentation					
Overall impact					

Feedback on team presentation check list

Rate each aspect of the team's presentation, scoring 1 where you think the presentation is totally unconvincing, fragmented and ineffective, up to 5 for a very convincing and effective team performance.

Dimension	1	2	3	4	5
How effectively did the team:					
1. Explain the objectives or purpose of the presentation.					
2. Introduce each presenter.					
3. Explain how questions from the audience would be managed.					
4. Use a clear structure for the presentation.					
5. Link the individual contributions together.					
6. Demonstrate they had rehearsed.					
7. Have a clearly defined team style.					
8. Support each other.					
9. Demonstrate they all knew the presentation content.					
10. Demonstrate they had reviewed spelling, quality of handouts.					
11. Present with confidence and impact.					
12. Achieve the objectives or purpose of the presentation.					

Note This check list can also be used by teams when planning a presentation, to identify which they think are the most important aspects of presentations. Each item shown above can be placed into a rank order of importance by the team, regardless of their order in this list.

Assertiveness check list

Consider the actions of the individual you are offering feedback to, and complete the following list. Be prepared to provide written notes and examples to support your position for each item.

Dimension	Always	Usually	Sometimes	Rarely	Never
You act in an authentic way by:					
1. Explaining to others what you want, in a calm, controlled way.	....	....	....	....	....
2. Giving and expecting to receive positive feedback.	....	....	....	....	....
3. Being prepared to negotiate so that everyone wins (i.e. a win–win strategy).	....	....	....	....	....
4. Not making assumptions, but continuing to check understanding.	....	....	....	....	....
5. Confronting problems as soon as possible – but retaining the option to return to these at an appropriate time.	....	....	....	....	....
You work within your own strengths by:					
6. Working within your own confidence, abilities and skills.	....	....	....	....	....
7. Being prepared to say where you stand on issues and what you think should be done.	....	....	....	....	....

Dimension	Always	Usually	Sometimes	Rarely	Never
8. Acting independently whenever possible.	....	....	....	....	....

You accept that others have rights to behave assertively by not:

	Always	Usually	Sometimes	Rarely	Never
9. Demanding what you want in a bullying, threatening, cajoling or sarcastic manner.	....	....	....	....	....
10. Infringing the rights of others.	....	....	....	....	....
11. Assuming others know what you want before you explain this to them.	....	....	....	....	....

Please note:

● Assertiveness can be developed just like any other skill.
● A truly assertive individual is an asset to any team, by creating a *win–win* environment for everyone concerned.

Reflective check list

Please complete this check list immediately after you have taken part in a game designed to develop team skills. It will then be collected, reissued at random, and the results will then be collated. This means that no one in the group will see your scoring, but that you will be able to see how your own responses differ from those of the group in general, if at all. In the checklist rating scale, 0 means 'not at all' and 5 means 'completely'. Thus there is no single 'right' response to any of the statements. Your replies simply represent your perception of events.

Dimension	0	1	2	3	4	5
As an individual, to what extent:						
1. Did you contribute ideas of your own?						
2. Did you explain/clarify/modify the ideas of others?						
3. Did you feel frustrated with members of your team?						
4. Did the team assist with your own learning processes?						
5. Do you now feel that you own the final solution your team produced?						

Dimension	0	1	2	3	4	5
From your observations of the team:						
6. Did the team create or develop ideas?						
7. Did team members assume roles (leader, chairman, scribe, etc.)?						
8. Did the team stop and listen to each other?						
9. Did the competitive spirit affect your team's approach to other groups?						
Consider the final result of your team efforts, and, given that you have a similar learning activity to achieve, to what extent would you:						
10. Wish to work with the same team?						
11. Want to direct a team towards your own ideas and ways of working?						
12. Prefer to work completely by yourself?						

Team development check list

Consider your team's performance during the recent game, and select (√) from the following list the six adjectives you think best describes this performance. If you cannot find suitable adjectives, add your own at the bottom of the page.

1.	Purposeful	.....	2. Considerate	.....
3.	Sensible	.....	4. Integrated	.....
5.	Willing	.....	6. Lethargic	.....
7.	Aimless	.....	8. Confused	.....
9.	Cheerful	.....	10. Directed	.....
11.	Miserable	.....	12. Workmanlike	.....
13.	Co-ordinated	.....	14. Busy	.....
15.	Stubborn	.....	16. Earnest	.....
17.	Intense	.....	18. Childlike	.....
19.	Sarcastic	.....	20. Destructive	.....
21.	Co-operative	.....	22. Competitive	.....
23.	Considerate	.....	24. United	.....
25.	Involved	.....	26. Concerted	.....
27.	Argumentative	.....	28. Enthusiastic	.....

| 29. | Creative | ..... | 30. | Playful | ..... |
| 31. | Curious | ..... | 32. | Supportive | ..... |

Your own adjectives
1.
2.
3.
4.
5.
6.

A design framework for team development programmes

Diagnostic	Development	Practice	Application
Aim The aim is to establish that there is a need for teams, and, if so, the current state of team development.	**Aim** The aim is to gain the commitment of all involved towards the growth and development of an effective team.	**Aim** The aim is to practise working as a team in a supportive environment where progress can be reviewed and evaluated.	**Aim** The aim is to apply the learning to the work environment.
Objectives The objectives are derived from the working environment, and are to: • Determine the level of interdependence in work roles within the organization;	**Objectives** The objectives are derived from the *content* of models, principles and techniques of team development. They would be presented as part of a structured course, usually including formal or	**Objectives** The objectives centre on the *processes* involved, such as offering feedback, presenting to a group, acting as the team leader, acting in an assertive way, using influence, and so on. Hence, in order to be	**Objectives** The objectives relate directly to work and are designed to focus on: • the effective changes which take place in the development of teams; • the increased commitment

Diagnostic	Development	Practice	Application
• ascertain changes taking place in the organizational work culture that may affect the need for team-working in the future; • identify the current stage of team development; • identify changes that could be made in the team to improve team performance; and • identify the learning or developmental needs of individuals.	informal presentations by the trainer. At the same time, the objectives would also help to strengthen the emergence of a team identity and commitment to the values of the team.	effective, a greater proportion of time and resources would need to be invested in this part of the programme than, for example, in the preceding stage.	of individuals; • cultural changes which are brought about by development of work teams; and • strategies and techniques for measuring and evaluating the effectiveness of teams at work.
Commentary Part of the diagnostic process would have been carried out prior to the planned development programmes. Individuals would take from these sessions a greater awareness of the interdependent nature of their work, and an awareness of the skills needed by themselves and others involved. The line manager and/or	**Commentary** The individual would take from these sessions a greater *understanding* and *knowledge* of the skills, and how they could be applied within their own work teams. The games and activities would be supported by formal and informal presentations covering team development models, and so on. If necessary, an assessment could be made of the	**Commentary** Individuals would take from these sessions a greater awareness of their own performance level, constructive advice on how to improve and so forth. Individuals could complete a personal action plan to record their own future development needs and actions planned, to be used in the next phase (*Application*) or in the work-place. The activities would be	**Commentary** These activities are designed to relate to the work situation, and could be carried out either during or after the course has taken place. They could be implemented in a number of ways. For example: • by the individual in discussion during performance reviews with the line manager; • by the individual as part of an NVQ/formal

270

colleagues may be asked to contribute to the information produced, in addition to the course participant. For example, through periodic appraisals and/or job performance interviews, line managers would be in a position to identify the learning and developmental needs of others.

The outcomes from the diagnostic stage could be used as part of an evaluation of the effectiveness of the course in:

• changing the level of knowledge; enhancing the awareness of the individual that they are part of a team;
• changing the individual's priorities in his or her own development; developing team plans for addressing training needs or for changing work practices, and so forth;
• bringing about behavioural changes that can bring benefits to the individual and the team.

effectiveness of the course by the use of written or oral questions to individuals.

supported by for example, formal presentations, simulations, case studies, recorded incidents taken from a work situation, and role play.

The emphasis is on helping individuals to develop team skills in a supportive and non-threatening environment. Feedback from the trainer and colleagues is an important part of the process.

qualification requirement;
• by the individual in discussion during team development meetings at work
• by the individual in subsequent discussion in formal/informal team development programmes.
• by colleagues in discussion during informal/formal team development sessions.

The Excellent Trainer

Putting NLP to Work

Di Kamp

Most trainers are familiar with the principles of Neuro Linguistic Programming. What Di Kamp does in her book is to show how NLP techniques can be directly applied to the business of training.

Kamp looks first at the fast-changing organizational world in which trainers now operate, then at the role of the trainer and the skills and qualities required. She goes on to deal with the actual training process and provides systematic guidance on using NLP in preparation, delivery and follow-up. Finally she explores the need for continuous improvement, offering not only ideas and explanation but also instruments and activities designed to enhance both personal and professional development.

If you are involved in training, you'll find this book a powerful tool both for developing yourself and for enriching the learning opportunities you create for others.

Gower

Handbook of Management Games and Simulations

Sixth Edition

Edited by Chris Elgood

What kinds of management games are there? How do they compare with other methods of learning? Where can I find the most suitable games for the training objectives I have in mind?

Handbook of Management Games and Simulations provides detailed answers to these questions and many others.

Part 1 of *the Handbook* examines the characteristics and applications of the different types of game. It explains how they promote learning and the circumstances for which they are best suited.

Part 2 comprises a detailed directory of some 300 games and simulations. Each one is described in terms of its target group, subject area, nature and purpose, and the means by which the outcome is established and made known. The entries also contain administrative data including the number of players, the number of teams and the time required. Several indexes enable readers to locate precisely those games that would be relevant for their own needs.

This Sixth edition has been revised to reflect recent developments. And of course the directory has been completely updated. Chris Elgood's *Handbook* will continue to be indispensable for anyone concerned with management development.

Gower

Handbook of
Technology-Based Training

Edited by Brian Tucker
The Forum for Technology in Training

Technology-based training (TBT) has moved a long way since the early days of computer-based training in the 1960s and 1970s. Today it offers a flexible, cost-effective way of meeting the ever increasing need for people to re-skill.

Handbook of Technology-Based Training provides an accessible guide to the potential benefits and pitfalls of this form of training. It describes the evolution of technology-based training; the various technologies and their uses; the benefits of using such flexible learning; the important issues of how to use the technology; how to implement TBT in an organization and where the future might lie. Brian Tucker also deals with choosing and evaluating generic training and the issues of bespoke training, either produced in-house or outsourced.

The *Handbook* is not highly technical, and deals with the issues in a readily understandable way. It uses examples and detailed case studies to demonstrate how nine leading organizations have managed the various issues and how they have benefited from this approach to training. These include Sun Life, Vauxhall, Lloyds Bank, Argos, British Gas and British Steel.

Structured in two parts, the first provides a complete overview of the subject. The second consists of a directory of over 700 generic TBT courseware titles, indexed by subject; title, medium, and producer. Each entry includes the title of the courseware, its purpose and suitability, a brief description, delivery methods, hardware requirements, price and supplier details.

Gower

Participative Training Skills

John Rodwell

It is generally accepted that, for developing skills, participative methods are the best. Here at last is a practical guide to maximizing their effectiveness.

Drawing on his extensive experience as a trainer, John Rodwell explores the whole range of participative activities from the trainer's point of view. The first part of his book looks at the principles and the 'core skills' involved. It shows how trainee participation corresponds to the processes of adult learning and goes on to describe each specific skill, including the relevant psychological models. The second part devotes a chapter to each method, explaining:

• what it is
• why and when it is used
• how to apply the core skills in relation to the method
• how to deal with potential problems.

A 'skills checklist' summarizes the guidelines presented in the chapter. The book ends with a comprehensive matrix showing which method is most suitable for meeting which objectives.

For anyone concerned with skill development *Participative Training Skills* represents an invaluable handbook.

Gower

75 Ways to Liven Up Your Training

A Collection of Energizing Activities

Martin Orridge

Most of the activities in Martin Orridge's book require little in the way of either expertise or equipment. Yet they provide a powerful way of stimulating creativity, helping people to enjoy learning, or simply injecting new momentum into the training process.

Each activity is presented under a standard set of headings, including a brief description, a statement of purpose, likely duration, a note of any materials required and detailed instructions for running the event. In addition there are suggestions for debriefing and possible variations.

To help users to select the most appropriate activities they are arranged in the book by type or process. There are exercises for individuals, pairs and large groups and they range from icebreakers to closing events.

Trainers, managers, team leaders and anyone responsible for developing people will find this volume a rich store-house of ideas.

Gower

Successful Communication Through NLP

A Trainer's Guide

Sally Dimmick

Most professional trainers nowadays have some understanding of Neuro Linguistic Programming. They probably know that people take in information about the world through a 'preferred representational channel' and that we communicate better with people if we use their preferred channel - visual, auditory or kinaesthetic. Sally Dimmick's book goes further. It shows how NLP principles can be applied to every aspect of training and which particular aids and methods are the most suitable for each channel.

The first part of the text outlines the main concepts of NLP and explains how to identify a person's preferred channel. It also looks briefly at the significance of learning styles. Part II examines each representational channel in turn and relates it to the corresponding training methods and materials. The final chapter provides ways of combining the channels so as to maximize the transfer of learning. The text is enlivened throughout by anecdotes, examples and illustrations.

For teachers, trainers, managers and indeed anyone faced with the need to communicate in a professional way, Sally Dimmick's guide will prove invaluable. It will be particularly welcomed by trainers looking for practical advice on how to use NLP.

Gower